Gideon D

THE PIRATES! In an A...

Fresh from their mishaps with Charles Darwin and the evil Bishop of Oxford, the Pirates set sail in a bouncy new vessel—purchased on credit. In order to repay his debts, the Pirate Captain is determined to capture the enigmatic White Whale, hunted by the notoriously moody Ahab, who has promised a reward.

Chaos ensues, featuring the lascivious Cutlass Liz; the world's most dangerous mosquito; an excerpt from the Pirate Captain's novel in progress (a bodice ripper, of course); whale ventriloquism; practical lessons in whale painting; a shanty-singing contest in a Las Vegas casino; and a dramatic climax in which the Pirate Captain's Prize Ham saves the day!

Move over, Herman Melville.

Gideon Defoe, who lives in London, is also the author of *The Pirates! In an Adventure with Scientists* and the forthcoming *The Pirates! In an Adventure with Communists* (Pantheon Books, 2006). Like all the English, he lives with his butler in a castle and spends most of his time having jousts.

Flip this book for *The Pirates! In an Adventure with Scientists* . . .

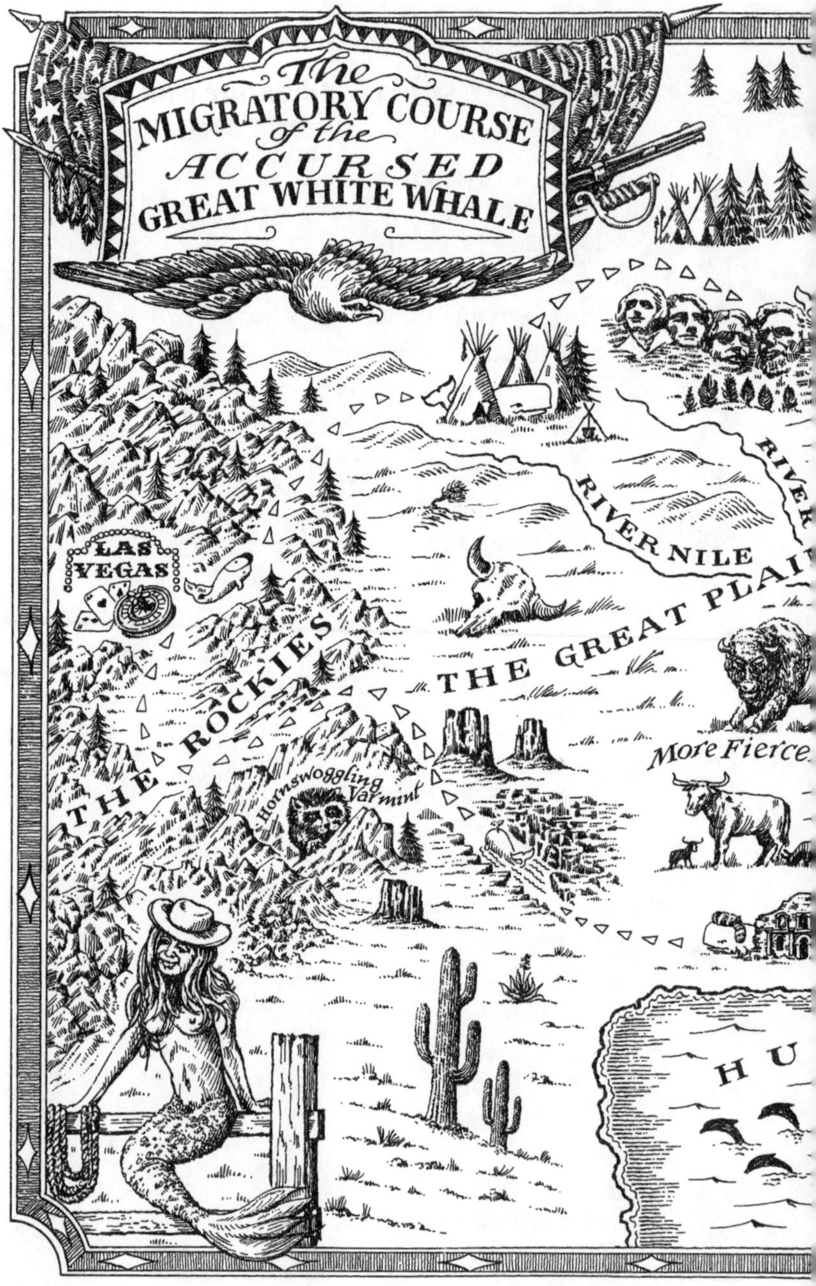

The MIGRATORY COURSE of the ACCURSED GREAT WHITE WHALE

LAS VEGAS

RIVER NILE

THE ROCKIES

THE GREAT

More Fierce

Hornswoggling Varmint

HE LAKE DISTRICT

VAST FOREST

Nantucket

Coney Island

FIERCE ANIMALS

Washington

The PIRATES in an Adventure with a MOSQUITO

THE BILLY HILLS

MAZON

N

als

Graceland

The Cotton Belt

Another Fierce Animal

lamo

SON

BAY

Cape Canaveral

DS '05

ALSO BY GIDEON DEFOE

The Pirates! In an Adventure with Scientists

THE PIRATES!

In an Adventure with Ahab

THE PIRATES!

In an Adventure with Ahab

Gideon Defoe

Vintage Books
A Division of Random House, Inc.
NEW YORK

FIRST VINTAGE BOOKS EDITION, JULY 2006

The Library of Congress has cataloged the Pantheon edition as follows:
Defoe, Gideon.
The pirates! : in an adventure with Ahab / Gideon Defoe.
p. cm.
1. Pirates—Fiction. 2. Ahab, Captain (Fictitious Character)—Fiction. 3. Whaling ships—Fiction. 4. Ship Captains—Fiction. 5. Whaling—Fiction. 6. Whales—Fiction I. Title.
PR6104.E525P567 2005
823'.92—dc22
2005045920

Vintage ISBN-10: 1-4000-7750-8
Vintage ISBN-13: 978-1-4000-7750-2

www.vintagebooks.com
www.gideondefoe.com

Printed in the United States of America
10 9 8 7 6 5 4 3 2

To Sophie,

who still has a quarter of a million pounds
of which I have not seen a single penny,
even though this is the second entire book
that I have dedicated to her.

CONTENTS

THE PIRATES!

In an Adventure with Ahab

One

I BATTLED A TON OF TURTLE!

'That one looks almost exactly like a whale!' 'No it doesn't. It looks like a pile of rags with an ant stood on them. But for some reason the ant only has five legs.'

'It's more like a cutlass. Or a beautiful mermaid lady.'

'It's a big seagull!'

'It's a skull!'

The pirates were busy lying on their backs on the deck of the pirate boat trying to decide what clouds looked like. Most days this enterprise would end up with the pirates having a brawl about whether a cloud would taste more like a marshmallow or a meringue if you could eat one, but today, before the pirates even had the chance to get their cutlasses out or pull angry faces at each other, there was a sudden crack, a shower of dust and splinters, and with a tremendous crash the boat's mast fell down on top of them.

The mast completely flattened the pirate who liked to show off how much he knew about wine, whilst the pirate with a hook for a hand found himself engulfed in a billowing white sail, and he was soon chasing the other pirates about, pretending to be a ghost. There was such a commotion none of the pirates even noticed the galley doors swing open and the Pirate Captain himself step out onto the deck. The Pirate Captain had taken to wearing a dashing maroon smoking jacket and a blousy white shirt that had most of the buttons undone to reveal the glossy hairs on his chest. His chest hairs were almost as well-conditioned as the hairs in his luxuriant beard, which many of the crew felt to be one of the seven wonders of the oceanic world. If the pirate crew had been asked to list the seven wonders of the oceanic world in full they would have confidently said, in ascending order: 1) the Lighthouse at Pharos; 2) the Colossus of Rhodes; 3) Lulworth Cove; 4) those jellyfish that light up; 5) Lobsters; 6) Girls In Bikinis; 7) the Pirate Captain's fantastic beard.

'What in blazes is going on, you oily wretches?!' the Pirate Captain bellowed.

The pirates all dusted themselves down, and the pirate with a hook for a hand sheepishly took off the sail and stopped doing ghost noises.

'Sorry, Captain,' said the pirate in green. 'We were just discussing what the clouds looked like when the mast fell down again.'

The Pirate Captain stepped over the bits of broken mast and tangled rigging and squinted up at the cloud that the pirates were looking at.[1] He clicked his tongue thoughtfully.

'It looks,' he said, after a little deliberation, 'like my stentorian nose with a bottle of grog next to it.'

The pirates all nodded, and slapped their foreheads, because that was *exactly* what the cloud most looked like, and they could all see it now the Pirate Captain had pointed it out.

'Listen, lads. Looking at clouds is all well and good,' said the Captain sternly, 'but some of us have important piratical work to do. So try and keep the noise down. Maybe tie a few knots, or something quiet like that.'

And with a waggle of his eyebrows and a wave of his cutlass, the Pirate Captain swept back through the big oak doors to his office. As

1 Clouds that look like things tend to be fair-weather cumulus clouds, which have a lifetime of just 5–40 minutes.

the doors slammed shut, one of them fell off its hinges, which slightly diminished the imperious effect he had been going for.

Back in his office the Pirate Captain sat at his desk and tried to get on with some work. As usual he spent a few minutes arranging his quills and paperweights. After that he tapped a pencil against his teeth. Then he tried balancing an inkpot on his nose. Finally he got up and walked around the room a little bit, hoping he might get some inspiration from the various portraits of himself that he had hung up about the place. He'd had some new ones done since their last adventure. There was a black-and-white painting that showed him with his shirt off tenderly cradling a baby. There was one of him emerging from an old boot alongside a giant kitten. And next to that was an actual 'Wanted' poster[2], which had a grainy picture of the Pirate Captain on it, and a bounty of ten thousand doubloons. The Pirate Captain stopped in front of a mirror and practised pulling the same face that he was doing in the Wanted poster, until a tentative knock at the door sent him diving back behind his desk. He scratched his forehead to show how deep in thought he was and said, 'Come in!' in his best working voice. The pirate with a scarf poked his head around the door.

'Hello Number Two,' said the Pirate Captain.

'Hello Pirate Captain,' said the pirate with a scarf, who for some reason was carrying the boat's steering wheel. 'I was hoping I could have a word?'

'Of course!' The Pirate Captain waved for him to take a seat. 'Actually, I'm glad you're here—you can help me with this work I'm doing.' He looked at his second-in-command seriously. 'I'm making a list of when it's acceptable for a pirate to cry.'

2 In 1718 the Governor of Virginia offered a reward of £100 for the capture of the notorious Blackbeard. That's about £10,769 in nowadays money, so it probably wouldn't have been worth the bother.

'That sounds very important, Captain,' said the pirate with a scarf, fiddling anxiously with his eye-patch. He had a delicate topic he wanted to broach, and you never could tell with the Captain if he might not fly into one of his terrible rages, because he prided himself on being unpredictable, like the ocean.

'So far I've got: one—when holding a seagull covered in oil. Two—when singing a shanty that reminds him of orphans. Three—when confronted by the unremitting loneliness of the human condition. Four—chops. I've just written the word "chops". Not really sure where I was going with that one. Any ideas?'

'It's a very good list, Captain,' said the pirate with a scarf, wondering why the last few zeros on the Captain's Wanted poster were in a different colour ink from the others. 'But there's something a few of the other pirates wanted me to ask you about.'

'Oh dear,' said the Pirate Captain, noticing the worried look on the scarf-wearing pirate's otherwise rugged face. 'Nothing relationship-based, I hope? You know how I'm not very good with emotional issues.' The Captain paused and looked out of the porthole. 'I think the problem is I'm just not very interested in them.'

'No, Captain. Nothing like that.'

'Well then. Fire away!'

'It's the boat, Captain. I don't know if you've noticed, and it would be fair enough if you hadn't, what with you being so busy making lists and all, but . . . well . . .' The scarf-wearing pirate tried to think of the most tactful way to put it. 'She's in a bit of a state.'

The Pirate Captain looked thoughtfully at the fraying wooden beams and the big patches of mould on the ceiling. 'Oh, I think "state" is a bit harsh. "Full of character" is probably the phrase you're after.'

'That's the third time this week the mast has fallen down, Captain.'

'Good thing too. Keeps the lads on their toes!'

'It's not just the mast, Captain,' the scarf-wearing pirate persisted. 'The cannons don't work properly. Several of the pirates have been getting nasty splinters, from the deck being so rotten. There's tar all over the place. And this,' he held up the boat's wheel and waggled it about, 'just came clean off in my hands.'[3]

'Arrrr.' The Pirate Captain stroked his beard. 'I suppose we need that for the . . . the uh . . .'

'Steering, sir. It moves the rudder.'

'Of course, the rudder. I knew that. The rudder's the one with the portholes, isn't it?'

'That's the forecastle, Captain.'

'Yes, the forecastle. Anyhow, pass it over here.' The Captain took the wheel, gave his trusty number two a reassuring wink, strode over to the back of his office and hung it on a spare nail that was sticking out from the wall. 'Paint a few numbers round the edge, it's got the makings of a nice dartboard, don't you think? Problem solved.'

Before the Pirate Captain had time to congratulate himself on this clever idea, the steering wheel thudded onto the carpet, taking the nail and a piece of the boat's wall with it. A spray of seawater jetted into the Captain's office and knocked an astrolabe off his mantelpiece. The Pirate Captain frowned.

'Look at that. It's made a little hole,' he said. But without missing a beat he picked up one of his portraits—the one of him smiling standing next to a lady-boy on the beach in Thailand—and propped it up over the leak.

'I don't think you can really just cover up holes with pictures, Captain,' said the pirate with a scarf sadly, as a steady stream of water went on dribbling down onto the carpet.

'Nonsense,' snorted the Pirate Captain, briefly pulling aside another painting to reveal a second nasty-looking gash in the wall. 'See. That's much worse, and it's been there for ages!'

The Pirate Captain grinned, but the pirate with a scarf just gave him a reproachful look.

---

3 The ship's wheel first replaced the tiller in 1705.

'The boat's really not safe, Captain. What if there was a storm? She wouldn't hold together for a minute.'

'I suppose a few of the lads might get washed out to sea,' agreed the Captain with a shrug. 'But, like my wise old Aunt Joan always says, it's a harsh life out on the ocean.'

'It's not just the pirates I'm thinking of,' said the scarf-wearing pirate. He paused meaningfully. 'What about your Prize Ham?'

He pointed at the big glass-fronted display case in the corner of the room. Inside the case hung the Pirate Captain's pride and joy—a huge glistening honey-roast ham.[4] It was about as close as you could get to the platonic ideal of a ham, if Plato had spent more time discussing hams and less time mucking about with triangles. It gleamed like a lumpy pink jewel where the sunlight from the port-hole caught its honey glaze. There was even a little silk bow tied around the thin end.

'Oh goodness,' said the Pirate Captain, looking lovingly at the ham. 'You're right. I don't think I could bear the thought of anything happening to her. And you know I can't say no when you do those big sad eyes at me.' He slumped back into his chair. 'What were you thinking?'

'We're not far from Nantucket, Captain,' said the pirate with a scarf, pointing at the nautical chart that the Captain had been using as a blotter.

'I know a limerick about Nantucket,' said the Pirate Captain brightly.

'It's where Cutlass Liz has her pirate boatyard,' said the pirate with a scarf, trying his best to keep the conversation on topic, which could be difficult with the Pirate Captain. 'I thought we might stop off and get the boat fixed up properly. Then after that we could have an adventure, maybe with spies or something.'

4 The most expensive ham in the world is *pata negra iberico* ham, which costs around £13 per 100 grams. Each pig spends its brief life feasting on 8 kg per day of the sweet, oily holm oak acorns found in the Mediterranean woodlands where they are raised.

'Hell's bells,' exclaimed the Pirate Captain. 'Cutlass Liz! The Butcher of Barbados. I don't think they hand out those sort of nick-names for no good reason.'

The pirate with a scarf nodded ruefully. 'It's pretty hard to find reputable boatyards that are prepared to deal with us pirates,' he pointed out.

'Yes, I suppose you're right. Sometimes I wonder if I should have taken up a more respectable line of work. Did I tell you how my mother was hoping I would be an architect?'

'I'm sure you'd have made a brilliant architect, Pirate Captain.'

'I'd have liked building those little models best. With the cut-out people.'

The Pirate Captain drifted off for a moment, thinking about his career choices.

In the boat's dining room the rest of the pirates were already tucking into their lunch. On board a pirate boat it wasn't considered rude to start before everybody was present, and you could even put your elbows on the table. Those were just two of the perks that attracted people to the piratical life. The Pirate Captain strode in followed by the pirate with a scarf to tell the crew the news. He picked up his 'Number One Boss' mug that the pirates had given him for his last birthday and downed it in one gulp. Then he banged the mug on the table.

'Listen up lads—and lady,' said the Pirate Captain with a nod to Jennifer, who had joined them on their last exciting adventure. 'What's the single most important thing in the life of a pirate?'

The crew all looked deep in thought. There were a few whispered discussions. Then the pirate in green put his hand up.

'Is it love?' he asked.

The Pirate Captain rubbed the back of his neck. 'Yes, all right. That's probably true. But after that, what's the next most important thing?'

'Respecting his or her mother?' suggested the pirate with gout.

'Fair enough,' conceded the Pirate Captain. 'You'd be nowhere without your mothers. But then what? What's the third most important thing?'

The crew looked stumped.

'His pirate boat!' roared the Captain. 'It's come to my attention that the old girl's a little past her best. And I can hardly maintain my reputation as a debonair terror of the High Seas with bits falling off the boat all the time, can I? So you'll be pleased to know that we're paying a visit to Cutlass Liz's boatyard.'

The pirates didn't look very pleased at all. Most of them looked petrified.

'Cutlass Liz!' exclaimed the sassy pirate.

'They say she's as deadly as she is beautiful!' said the pirate in green.

'I heard she ate twenty babies, just to show her crew how ruthless she was!' said the albino pirate.

'Twenty whole babies all in one sitting!'

'You tried that once, didn't you, Pirate Captain? To terrify that admiral?'

'But there weren't any babies around at the time.'

'I remember that. We drew faces on a load of hams instead. Ham babies!' A few of the pirates laughed as they remembered their adventure with the ham babies. Then they remembered about Cutlass Liz and looked worried again.

'Oh, I'm sure her reputation has been exaggerated,' said the Pirate Captain, helping himself to another mug of grog. 'You know how us pirates get. She's probably just a bit stroppy now and again. And besides—who *hasn't* slit a man's belly open for looking at them cockeyed?'

Two

SKULL HUNT ON PYGMY ISLAND!

And so the pirate boat arrived at the island of Nantucket. Sailing past the harbour, it struck the pirates that the whole place seemed slightly one-note.[5] The quayside inns all had names like 'The Blue Whale's Rest' or 'The Narwhal's Arms', and everywhere you looked there were big bronze statues of grimacing whales with harpoons sticking out of their sides and stalls that only seemed to sell 'I Had A *Blubberly Time* In Nantucket' T-shirts and tatty-looking snowstorms with whales in them. They pulled up alongside Cutlass Liz's boatyard, and the Pirate Captain couldn't help but notice how shabby the pirate boat looked parked next to all the shiny new pirate boats that lined the side of the dock. He hoped that the holes in her hull and bits of rigging held together by tape would say 'rustic charm' rather than 'barely afloat'. There was a sign hung on the boatyard gate:

5 In the early nineteenth century Nantucket was the whaling capital of the world. Whaling voyages would set out from port in search of 'greasy luck', which apparently the whalers could say without laughing.

CUTLASS LIZ!
PIRATE BOATS USED & NEW
NO DOGS, ROYAL NAVY OR SENSITIVE TYPES

The pirates looked around, but apart from some seagulls kicking about and a couple of unkempt old men shouting prophetic tales of doom at sea to nobody in particular, the place seemed deserted.

'Looks like she's not about,' said the albino pirate. 'Might as well be going.'

'Yes, we did our best,' said the pirate in green.

'No point dilly-dallying,' said the pirate with gout.

The Pirate Captain was just about to ask if they were pirates or pignuts, when Cutlass Liz made her dramatic entrance. In his time the Pirate Captain had made a number of dramatic entrances of his own—not always intentional it had to be said, as quite often they were the result of him accidentally setting himself on fire—but even he had to admit that Cutlass Liz's dramatic entrance set an extremely high dramatic-entrance standard. A terrified-looking man in a tattered coat came sprinting desperately across the cobblestones. He stopped for a moment, stared wildly about, looked up, and shrieked. The pirates all looked up too, just in time to see Cutlass Liz come sliding down the mainsail of one of the boats, swing across the dock on a piece of rigging, and land with an athletic somersault right in front of the terrified-looking man, who she lifted off his feet by one ear. Cutlass Liz changed the colour of her hair as often as the Pirate Captain ate mixed grills, but at the moment it was a vivid red, which went well with the bloodstains on her blouse. She didn't have a luxuriant beard, but otherwise she cut quite the piratical dash: a huge sapphire necklace that spelt 'LIZ' hung around her neck, and in her belly button she wore a gigantic diamond shaped like a skull, which was rumoured to have been a gift from Napoleon, who she had dated briefly as a teenager. On any other pirate, the necklace and the diamond together might have looked a little bit much, but Cutlass Liz was famed for having the best face in the entire eastern seaboard, and so she somehow carried it off. If he had been meeting her a hundred and fifty years later, the Pirate Captain might have been struck by how much Cutlass Liz looked like the actress Julie Christie from around the time of *Billy Liar* or maybe *Darling*, but he wasn't, so he just thought she looked fantastic. The pirate with a scarf sighed, because he knew how the Pirate Captain tended to get around attractive women.

'I can pay, Cutlass! I can pay! One more day!' pleaded the man with a tattered coat.

'Too late, Jericho Leith,' said Cutlass Liz, grinning from ear to ear. 'Two minutes too late!'

And with that, she took out her cutlass and did some unspeakable things to the unfortunate Jericho Leith. The Pirate Captain stood and watched politely, occasionally wiping a bit of blood from his eyes. Finally, just when he was starting to think that it might go on all day, Jericho Leith let out a horrifying gurgle and slumped down dead. Cutlass Liz deftly kicked his body into the harbour, and turned on her heel to face the pirates.

'You must be Cutlass Liz,' said the Pirate Captain, doffing his hat[6] and doing a little bow. 'I'm the Pirate Captain. You've probably heard of me. Possibly from one of those libellous accounts of my adventures that seem to be doing the rounds. I'm a successful pirate, you know.'

'Is that a fact?' Cutlass Liz arched a perfectly shaped eyebrow, and went on wiping customer innards off her hands with a flannel.

'Oh yes. I lead an extremely glamorous lifestyle,' said the Pirate Captain, hoping she had noticed how many of his best lace ribbons he had tied in his beard that morning. 'And I'm really very well off. Because of all the treasure.'

6 The piratical tri-corn hat evolved from the 'cocked hat' worn in the English Civil War, where one side of a wide-brimmed hat was tipped up to allow firing of a musket from the shoulder.

The pirate with a scarf bit his lip. This wasn't the first time he had heard the Pirate Captain be a bit less than honest about his financial status when talking to a lady.

'I've got more treasure chests than I know what to do with,' continued the Captain. 'All fit to bursting with silvery doubloons and pearls and sapphires and rubies, and those green ones too.'

'Emeralds?'

'Yes, that's it, emeralds. Buckets of emeralds. It's a wonder the boat can even move.'

'Tell me,' said Cutlass Liz, 'what kind of pirate captain doesn't have a crew?'

The Pirate Captain looked about and realised that apart from the pirate with a scarf, his crew were nowhere to be seen.

'Aarrrr. It's just they're all a little bit scared of you,' said the Pirate Captain apologetically. 'Come on, you coves!'

The pirates reluctantly slunk out from behind various barrels and piles of old fish. Several of them held their hands over their faces in the mistaken belief that if they couldn't see Cutlass Liz then she couldn't see them.

'You know I once ate twenty babies?' said Cutlass Liz, looking them up and down. The crew all nodded fearfully.

'I'm sure babies taste a lot better than pirates,' said the albino pirate. 'Because they'd be fresher. And not as salty.'

Cutlass Liz stared incredulously at the albino pirate. The albino pirate was so frightened that he somehow managed to go even whiter than usual. For a moment nobody said a thing. Then Cutlass Liz threw back her head and let out a laugh that sounded like a delicate foghorn. She pinched one of the albino pirate's cheeks and slapped him hard on the back. 'I like you. I don't know what you are, but I like you. What are you? Some kind of a milk bottle?'

'I don't think so,' said the albino pirate, trembling.

'Well you're all right. I suppose you swabs are here to get your boat fixed up?' said Cutlass Liz, putting her hands on her hips.

'Yes, please. I mean to say, if that would be all right. Not if you're too busy or anything,' said the scarf-wearing pirate.

Cutlass Liz looked at the ramshackle old pirate boat and frowned. 'Is that a piece of *gammon* you've patched up the side with?'

'You'd be surprised how effective a properly cooked bit of gammon can be at keeping out the weather,' explained the Pirate Captain, making sure to touch his hair, because he remembered hearing that touching your own hair was a good way to be flirtatious with someone.

'And she seems to be listing rather badly.'

'Oh, that's just because I like to keep my boats at a jaunty angle. It's to demonstrate that I don't take life too seriously.'

'Not having a mast? Does that demonstrate anything in particular?'

'Ah, no. Not as such.'

'Sorry, boys,' said Cutlass Liz with a shrug. 'I don't think there's much I can do for her. But have you thought about trading her in? I do part exchange, you know.'

'How much do you think the old girl's worth?' asked the pirate in green.

'She's sturdier than she looks,' lied the scarf-wearing pirate.

'Yes. And you're not just getting a boat,' said the sassy pirate. 'I reckon there must be about five hundred pounds of barnacles stuck to her hull. That's got to be worth a bit.'[7]

'And it's full of rats,' added the albino pirate helpfully. He was going to say about the mushrooms that were growing out of the carpet in the galley as well, but the Pirate Captain cut in before he had a chance.

'She's not on fire. That's got to count for something.'

'Well . . .,' Cutlass Liz tapped the pirate boat's hull with her boot,

---

7 The cement exuded by barnacles is an extremely tough protein polymer. It is twice as strong as the epoxy glue used on the space shuttle. Also, the barnacle penis is ten times as long as the rest of its body.

and it made a sort of squelching noise. 'You're robbing me, but I could probably stretch to fifty doubloons. Might get some useful kindling out of her. What are you looking to replace it with?' She waved at the various types of boat that were sat about her boatyard. 'I've got pirate sloops, pirate galleons, pirate yachts, pirate schooners, pirate pedalos . . . anything take your fancy?'

'I was thinking something to match my fearsome and larger-than-life personality,' said the Pirate Captain. 'I like the look of that big one over there.'

Cutlass Liz nodded approvingly. 'The *Lovely Emma*? She can outrun anything in the Royal Navy, and short of being attacked by a sea monster, that double-layered hull makes her virtually unsinkable. And there's plenty of room for all that treasure of yours.'

The pirates all looked up at the *Lovely Emma*. The pirate with a scarf counted a full thirty gleaming cannons. Some of the less practically minded pirates noticed she had the most striking figurehead they had ever seen—a smiling lady carved out of oak. From the waist up the smiling lady left almost nothing to the imagination, and several of the younger pirates' eyes grew as wide as saucers.

'Yes, that's the kind of thing we're after. How much does she cost? After you've knocked off the fifty doubloons, that is?'

'Six thousand doubloons.'

The Pirate Captain almost dropped his cutlass. He took a moment to compose himself and pretended to be thinking it over.

'It's a bit flash, is the thing. I don't want people thinking I'm vulgar. How about that one over there?'

'That's the *Perch*. She's only five hundred doubloons,' said Cutlass Liz. 'And she comes with a free ham.'

'Aaarrr. Still a bit on the showy side. What about that one?' said the Pirate Captain, pointing disappointedly to the smallest boat in the lot.

'The *Sea Slug*? Two hundred doubloons.'

Before the Pirate Captain had time to say that maybe he wasn't that bothered about buying a new boat at all, mainly because of unspecified environmental concerns he had about them, he was interrupted by a shout from the other end of the docks.

'If it isn't my old friend the Pirate Captain!' bellowed a familiar voice. The Pirate Captain froze. All the blood drained from his face, though you wouldn't really notice this because of his luxuriant beard. But if beards had blood in them, it would have drained from that as well.

'Black Bellamy!' said the Pirate Captain, thinking that his day couldn't get much worse. Black Bellamy was the roguish rival pirate who the pirates had most recently encountered in their adventure with scientists. He was famous for having a beard that went up to his eyeballs and a matching rakish charm. There were several reasons why the Pirate Captain and Black Bellamy didn't get on, but the main one was that Black Bellamy was the Pirate Captain's evil nemesis, which obviously put quite a strain on the relationship.

'Buying yourself a new boat?' said Black Bellamy, beaming. 'Not before time!'

The Pirate Captain scowled. 'What are you doing here, you cove?'

'You know, whenever we meet you're always calling me a cove or a fiend or something terrible like that. A pirate's feelings could be quite hurt. I'm just picking up a few piratical supplies from Lizzie here. That the one you're getting?' Black Bellamy looked over at the *Sea Slug* and pulled a face. 'She's very nice. Compact. I think the French call it *bijou*. Sometimes I find all the space on the *Barbary Hen* such a burden. So much easier to keep something as small as that tidy.'

'As a matter of fact,' the Pirate Captain said with a sniff, 'I'm buying this one.' And he pointed straight at the *Lovely Emma*. The pirate with a scarf buried his face in his hands.

'Goodness,' said Black Bellamy, obviously impressed. 'The pirating business must be treating you well. I'm surprised there's so much money in, what was it . . .? Zoological specimens?'

'Yes, I've been meaning to have a word with you about that.'

'An honest mistake,' said Black Bellamy, holding his hands up with a cheeky shrug.

'You won't be disappointed with her, Pirate Captain,' said Cutlass Liz, giving him a playful tug on his beard. 'How do you plan to pay? Doubloons or treasure?'

The Pirate Captain paused. 'Aaarrrr. Thing is, all my treasure is a little tied up at the moment. It might take me a couple of weeks to get my hands on it.'

'Didn't you say it was all in treasure chests? On board your boat?'

'I did. That's to say, it is. But, uh, I have about a hundred treasure chests,' said the Pirate Captain, thinking on his feet, 'and that means about a hundred different keys. Obviously, for security purposes, I don't label either of them. So there's no knowing which key fits which chest.'

The Pirate Captain was quite pleased with this explanation, but Cutlass Liz just frowned.

'It shouldn't take too long to open one chest?'

'You'd think that, wouldn't you?' said the Pirate Captain. 'But—ah—you're working on the assumption that I try the chests in some sort of systematic order. Whereas what I'll actually do is try random keys in random chests, making no real note of which chest or which key I have already tried. It could take days.'

Cutlass Liz gave the Pirate Captain a look. It was the same sort of look as Jennifer sometimes gave him when he said he hadn't realised the boat's shower was occupied.

'You're not a time-waster, are you, Pirate Captain?' said Cutlass Liz, turning a pretty shade of pink round her décolletage. 'Because I save my most terrible cutlass work for time-wasters. Time-wasters and actors.'

'Can I just say,' said the Captain, deciding to change tack, 'that I've always approved of women at sea. A lot of pirates will tell you that the closest girls should get to nautical matters is making seaweed albums, or those boxes covered in shells. But I don't think that at all.'

Cutlass Liz tapped the blade of her cutlass.

'All right,' said the Pirate Captain with a sigh. 'I wasn't being entirely honest with you. My boat isn't actually full of bulging treasure chests.'

The Pirate Captain was dimly aware that this was the point in the adventure where he had the opportunity to come clean, and at the risk of a slightly wounded pride he and the crew could spend the next couple of weeks just sitting about Nantucket, chewing opium and taking naps. But he looked at the smirk playing across Black Bellamy's face and he looked at Cutlass Liz's fantastic cheekbones, and somehow the confession stuck in his craw.

'The truth of the matter,' the Pirate Captain found himself saying, 'is that the treasure chests aren't on my boat. Because they're buried on one of the Cayman Islands. For tax purposes.'[8]

Black Bellamy stifled a laugh, and Cutlass Liz puffed out her cheeks and weighed up the Captain and his rag-tag crew with a steely stare.

'I wouldn't normally do this, Pirate Captain,' she finally said, 'but you have a pleasant, open face. And I like your little milk-bottle man.'

Cutlass Liz disappeared into her office for a moment.

'Lovely girl, that Cutlass,' said Black Bellamy with a wink to the Pirate Captain. 'There's something really irresistible about a woman who can kill a man with just a pork loin, don't you think?'

'Haven't you got to go and be diabolical somewhere?' replied the Captain with a grimace.

Black Bellamy grinned again and looked at his pocket watch. 'I won't take that to heart, because I know you don't mean it. And I'm sure we'll be seeing each other again soon. So, till next time then.' With a bow and a wave to all the pirates Black Bellamy sauntered back down the dock, humming a cheery little shanty to himself as he went.

When Cutlass Liz reappeared from her office she was carrying a

8 Legend has it that in 1788 Caymanians rescued the crews of a Jamaican merchant ship convoy which had struck a reef at Gun Bay and that they were rewarded with King George III's promise never again to impose any tax.

stack of papers the size of a ship's log. She handed them to the Pirate Captain.

'You'll just need to sign this.'

The Pirate Captain leafed through the contract as his crew crowded around. 'This bit about cutting off my luxuriant beard if I default on the first payment. Is that really necessary?' said the Pirate Captain, wincing.

'And the paragraph describing how you'll hunt us down across the Seven Seas, and gut us like fishes. That seems needlessly graphic,' said the pirate with a scarf.

Cutlass Liz smiled sweetly, and waved at the array of skulls she had scattered about the boatyard. Most of them looked about the size and shape of the average pirate head.

'It's all standard terms and conditions,' she said, handing the Captain a quill which, if he didn't know better, looked as if it had been dipped in blood.

Three

I KNIFED MY WAY TO A DIAMOND PIT!

The Pirate Captain and the scarf-wearing pirate stood on the dock staring at a gigantic glass egg timer. Cutlass Liz had been very helpful in supplying it to the pirates and making clear exactly what it was for. 'Before this runs out, you boys bring me the full balance owing,' she had said, 'otherwise I'll enact section six, paragraph four. But I will be using a harpoon instead of an axe, to add a bit of local colour.' She had also taken great pride in letting them know that the grains in the egg-timer weren't grains of sand, but pieces of ground-up pirate bones. On their way back to clear out the old boat the pirate with a scarf tried to make some small talk about how you didn't seem to find the same quality of cannonball about nowadays, but the Pirate Captain could tell he was just trying to take his mind off their predicament.

'Feisty lass, that Cutlass Liz, isn't she, Number Two?' said the Pirate Captain, packing away his portraits in an old wooden trunk.

'You could put it like that,' said the pirate with a scarf dubiously.

'I suppose you noticed the frisson between us?' added the Pirate Captain. 'That was sexual tension. I think she was quite impressed by me.'

The pirate with a scarf nodded. The Pirate Captain was a master of understanding body language, and he often detected things that nobody else would have picked up on.

The Pirate Captain clicked the trunk shut and beckoned for a couple of the crew to take it across to the *Lovely Emma*. Then he began to flick through the boat's inventory, to make sure that nothing got left behind. It didn't make for jaunty reading:

24 limes
1 Prize Ham
18 dry cured hams
2 boxes of ship's biscuits (one set custard cream/one bourbon)
4 barrels of tar
5 emergency doubloons taped to the underside of the teapot
1 pirate with an accordion (deceased and subsquently electroplated)

'It *is* just possible I got a little carried away, Number Two,' he said. 'We don't actually have any loot whatsoever, do we?'

'Not really, sir. We have several limes.'

The Pirate Captain ran a concerned hand through his luxuriant beard. 'I knew I was exaggerating our finances, but I had no idea things were in quite such a sorry state.'

'We do have that big stone coin, Captain. I think that's worth something on one of the more remote Pacific island economies.'[9]

Whilst the crew busied themselves moving everything into the new boat, the Pirate Captain went and sat on the edge of the dock, next to

9 If you are a fan of ridiculous oversized currency made out of big rolls of feathers and the like, then the Pitt Rivers Museum in Oxford is a great place to visit. Whilst you're there be sure to check out the shrunken heads that you will find downstairs in a display case next to some old violins.

the strips of gelatinous jellyfish bladders left out for salting. He whistled a little tune to himself and wondered where on earth he was going to find six thousand doubloons. A swarthy cove came and sat down next to him, and for one horrible moment the Pirate Captain thought he was going to be propositioned, because a surprising amount of that sort of thing went on amongst these sailor types. But rather than a saucy wink or a pinch on his seafaring behind, the man just offered him a swig of drink. He was a fearsome-looking fellow, with an ugly scar running the length of one cheek, and a stump of whale ivory poking out of his trousers instead of the more regular leg. But he was offering grog, so it seemed only right to be friendly.

'Call me Pirate Captain,' said the Pirate Captain, shaking his hand.

'Aaarrr,' said the stranger. 'The name's Ahab.'

And with that the man went back to staring at the black waves, almost as if he was looking for something. The Pirate Captain wasn't very good at sharing a comfortable silence with someone, unless it was a girl he had been seeing for a while. And even then, once the friendly feminine chatter had lapsed for too long, he tended to babble on about how much he liked the smell of their hair. So after a couple of awkward minutes he tried to kick-start the conversation.

'So. Ahab. You off anywhere interesting?'

'The whale,' the man murmured. 'I'm going to find myself the whale. I've charted the course he takes, and I'll sail to the ends of the earth if I have to. Typhoons, hurricanes, craggy rocks . . . Why, if the sea itself rose up against me, Ahab would not be stopped in his ungodly quest.'

'Wow. You must really like whales.'

'Not exactly,' said Ahab, his gaze still fixed on the sea. 'It was a whale that did this,' and he pointed at his ivory leg.

'A whale made you a prosthetic leg?' exclaimed the Pirate Captain, a little incredulously. 'But how? They don't have hands, do they? Just little flippers.'

'I meant it was the whale that left me without a leg. It was a man in Bedford gave me a new one.'

'Oh. I got bitten by a mosquito once,' offered the Pirate Captain. 'Look here—you can still see the bump. Well, you can't see it now, but a week ago it was the size of a golf ball.'

'I've never forgiven the brute,' snarled Ahab. 'And I mean to hunt him down to his watery grave.'

'Well, I've never forgiven that mosquito. But you can't spend your life chasing after a mosquito, can you?'

'He was white, Pirate Captain. White as snow. And monstrous big.'

'Goodness. I'm not sure I can really remember what that mosquito looked like at all. I mean to say, I don't know if I could pick him out in some sort of identity parade.'

'I'll have my vengeance!' spat Ahab, boiling with a tremendous fury. He looked as if he was about to hit something, but seemed to settle for just pulling an angry face. After a moment the strange man slapped the Pirate Captain on the back, stood up and turned to go.

'Good hunting, Pirate Captain!' said the mysterious fellow.

'Yes, and you,' said the Pirate Captain, a bit puzzled by the whole encounter. He wandered thoughtfully back to the *Lovely Emma*.

'Are we good to go, Number Two?' asked the Pirate Captain.

'Aye aye, Captain,' said the pirate with a scarf.

'Tell me something. Do you remember that mosquito, attacked me near Mozambique?'

'Erm, no. Not really, Captain.'

'Aaarrrr, well, that will be because I was so stoic about it, I hardly made any fuss. Big brute he was. Might even have been a queen. Do mosquitos have queens?'

'I think that's bees, Pirate Captain.'

'This wasn't a bee. It was definitely a mosquito—sucked my blood right out, like a ghoul. Anyhow, perhaps I went a little easy on the thing?'

'You've always been the magnanimous type, Captain.'

'You don't think it makes me look soft?'

'No, sir. Gentlemanly.'

Four

A SLOW BOAT TO BLOODSHED!

'It even comes with its own meat slicer,' said the pirate in green, flicking through the *Lovely Emma*'s brochure. 'Apparently it cuts ham so wafer-thin you can see through the slices! Imagine that! You could put ham all over your eyes and still see where you were going!'

'And it has proper beds, with mattresses!' said the albino pirate happily. 'No more falling out of stupid hammocks all the time.'

The pirates were all very excited by their new boat. Some of them thought the best thing about the *Lovely Emma* was its fancy on-board plumbing. Some of them thought the best things were the cannon covers made from ermine and pressed swans. Some of them thought the best thing was the ornamental garden. The Captain thought the best thing was probably the huge network of speaking tubes that ran around the length of the boat, because it meant he could talk to the crew or sing them a shanty whenever he felt like it, even if it was in the middle of the night. But whatever the best thing about the boat was, the pirates all agreed that the *Lovely Emma* was brilliant.

In his brand-new office the Pirate Captain pressed a button under his brand-new desk and watched as a shiny mahogany cupboard slid open. A little wooden monkey poured out a cup of grog and then did a clumsy mechanical dance, before disappearing back inside the cupboard. The Pirate Captain chuckled, drank the grog and then pressed the button over and over again, so that it looked like the wooden monkey was having an epileptic fit. He had just finally broken the monkey when the pirate in green came in with his afternoon tea.

'Tea, Captain,' said the pirate in green.

'Lovely,' said the Pirate Captain. 'Grog is all well and good, but it doesn't really beat a nice cup of tea.'

The pirate in green started to pour it out, but his hands were shaking and he ended up spilling most of the tea over the Captain's desk.

'Sorry, Captain. I'm not myself,' said the pirate in green, wiping the mess up with his sleeve.

'Something on your mind?'

'Don't get me wrong, Captain. It's great to have a nice new boat. It's just a couple of us pirates were thinking six thousand doubloons is an awful lot of money for us to come by in one adventure. And the getting cut to bits business . . . I don't much fancy the sound of that.'

'You know something?' said the Pirate Captain. 'For a moment there I would have agreed with you. It occurred to me that I might have been a touch rash saddling us with such a large debt. But sat here, looking at the way all this wood panelling brings out the russet hues of my beard, I've realised that *not* to have bought this boat would have been *false economy*. And you know what I'm always saying—the pirate's worst enemy is false economy. Even more so than the Royal Navy.'

Because the pirate in green didn't have the Pirate Captain's firm grasp of economics, he wasn't sure he understood the exact way in which false economy worked, but he vaguely remembered that it tended to crop up a lot when the Pirate Captain was shopping for meat and fancied treating himself to something from the butcher's *Finest* range.

'Besides, she looks a lot happier there, doesn't she?' said the Pirate Captain, nodding at his Prize Ham, which was now hung proudly in its case above the fireplace.

'She definitely goes very well with the lush carpeting,' agreed the pirate in green.

'Have I ever told you how I first came across the old dear?'

In fact the Pirate Captain had told the pirates his Prize Ham's origin story on several occasions, though it seemed to change every time. Depending on the Captain's mood the ham was either: an offering from a dying Aztec king; stolen from inside the tomb of a pharaoh; won in a duel with a samurai; the reincarnation of a gypsy princess; or a Christmas present from his Aunt Joan. The pirate in green was actually rather relieved that before the Pirate Captain could elaborate any further the sensible tones of the pirate with a scarf came wafting down the speaking tube to tell them that there was something up on deck that they should see.

For a moment after bounding up onto the deck the Pirate Captain wasn't sure what it was that the pirate with a scarf had called him for, but then he looked up and saw the thing.

'Oooh! An albatross! I think they're supposed to be lucky, aren't they?' said the Pirate Captain, squinting up at the majestic bird which was flying in little circles around the mast.

'Actually, sir, the albatross is traditionally seen as a symbol of oppressive burden or hindrance,' said the pirate in red.[10] It was a credit to the Captain's self-control that the pirate in red didn't get a cutlass in his eye right there and then.

'It has something tied to its leg, Captain.'

'So it has. What do you suppose it could be?'

'Perhaps it's a treasure map!'

'Let's throw our cutlasses at it!' said the Pirate Captain.

A few of the pirates threw their cutlasses at the albatross, but it

10 The albatross can live for up to eighty years, and it has the largest wingspan of any bird, often exceeding eleven and a half feet.

easily swooped out of the way, the cutlasses clattered back onto the deck and everybody had to scatter to avoid getting run through. Jennifer muttered something about how the Pirate Captain ought to think his plans through a little more. The Pirate Captain looked up at the albatross and narrowed his eyes.

'We're going to have to lure it down here somehow,' he said, a wily look coming over his face. 'One of you lubbers go fetch me some hens from the kitchen.'

The sassy pirate drew the short straw and he was soon rolling around in a puddle of pirate tar. Then all the other pirates took turns to throw some freshly plucked hen feathers at him, until he was covered from head to toe. He got a bit cross because a few of the feathers went in his mouth. Then the pirate who was good at origami folded his scarf into the shape of a beak, and they attached it with a rubber band to the sassy pirate's face. Jennifer fetched her lipstick and drew a lovely pair of sexy lady albatross lips on the sassy pirate's new beak. The sassy pirate already had naturally long eyelashes like a girl, so they didn't need to do anything with those.

'Make some sexy albatross noises,' said the Pirate Captain. 'And flap your arms a bit.'

The sassy pirate clearly didn't know what a sexy lady albatross sounded like, but he did his best. 'Caw! Caw!' he said through his origami scarf-beak. 'I'm a sexy lady albatross!'

It did the trick, and the other—genuine—albatross flapped down towards him, a frisky look in its avian eye. But before the lusty bird could put any albatross moves on the sassy pirate, the Pirate Captain leapt forward and covered it with a big sack. A few cutlass prods and some squawking later and the albatross lay dead on the floor.

'Look, Captain! It was a lady albatross all along!'

'Well. Who's to say albatrosses can't enjoy a touch of the Sapphic?' said the Pirate Captain reasonably. The crew all crowded around as the pirate with a scarf slipped a soggy piece of parchment from the bird's leg.

'Here's a stroke of luck!' said the Pirate Captain. 'It's a letter from Calico Jack, my old mentor at pirate academy.'

The Pirate Captain began to read the letter out loud:

> *'Dear Pirate Captain,*
> *I hope all is well and that you're not hanging in irons or anything. I'm writing to you from my sickbed, where I am suffering terribly with a kidney stone the size of a grapefruit. Such a common risk for us pirates, given our fondness for rich meats of all descriptions.'* [11]

Several of the crew shook their heads sadly, and more than one made a mental note to cut back on the feasts.

> *'I fear that my days of plundering and shouting things like 'I am a pirate!' may well be drawing to a close. So I wanted to tell you one thing—Pirate Captain, you were always my favourite pupil. Certainly you were much better than the others in your class, who I regarded merely as a brain, an athlete, a basket case, a princess and a criminal. I especially liked your commanding voice, stentorian nose, piercing blue eyes and firm grasp of nautical matters.*
>
> *Even as I write I can feel additional calculi agglomerating in my urinary tract, so I must be brief. Long story short, I believe that you, more than anybody, deserve to learn my greatest secret: for as a young pirate I discovered nothing less than the ultimate treasure, which I buried for safekeeping on an island just off the Florida Keys. The map is enclosed.*
>
> *Stay lucky,*
> *Calico Jack'* [12]

11 Kidney stones are a conglomeration of crystals (called calculi) in the kidney and bladder, which are exacerbated by high levels of uric acid. Meat, rhubarb, spinach, cocoa, pepper, nuts, and tea have been linked with stone formation, as well as insufficient intake of fluids.
12 A letter like this would probably have been known as a 'booty call'.

'Does the letter really say all that about you having a commanding voice and piercing eyes?' said the pirate in red, peering over the Pirate Captain's shoulder. 'I can't see that bit anywhere.'

The Pirate Captain glowered at the pirate in red, rolled up the letter and put it in his pocket. He turned to his second-in-command and grinned.

'You see? You worry too much. I told you something would come up.'

The pirates were all excited by what the ultimate treasure might turn out to be. The albino pirate thought that it would probably be the world's biggest necklace, whilst the pirate in green thought it would be a diamond so massive you couldn't even fit it into your mouth, and a few of the others were convinced it would be One Million Pounds.

'Whatever it turns out to be,' said the Pirate Captain, trying to calm his crew down a bit, 'it's sure to be enough to pay for the boat, and keep us in hooks and buckles for years to come. And if there's any left over, well, you know me . . . I'll probably give it to charity. Amputee pirates. Or maybe to some sort of creature sanctuary. You've got to give something back, haven't you?'

The pirates all nodded solemnly.

'Don't just stand about, lads. Brace the jib and hoist the mainsail and—uh—do all those things that make the boat go,' said the Pirate Captain, striding towards his office. 'With any luck, by this time tomorrow we'll be drinking champagne[13] from the smalls of ladies' backs! Except for Jennifer, of course. You can drink champagne from the small of a beefcake's back. Well, not just Jennifer, any of you can if you go for that sort of thing. I'm open-minded like that.'

The pirates had been digging for hours. Their muscles ached and the sweat streamed in torrents down their backs and faces. The stinging tropical sun rendered them speechless.

[13] During the early nineteenth century, up to forty per cent of champagne bottles exploded before even leaving the vineyard.

'You're doing a great job, lads!' said the Pirate Captain, sat a little way away under a stylish skull-and-crossbones parasol. He washed down a slice of ham with a swig of pirate grog. 'I just wish I could help. But you know what happens when I get sand in my beard—I could be out of action for days.'

The pirate in red wiped a soggy neckerchief across his brow and leant on his spade for a moment. 'Are you sure this is the spot, Captain?' he asked.

'Yes. Can't be long now! Chop, chop!' said the Pirate Captain, trying to be firm.

'You've got the treasure map the right way round this time?'

The Pirate Captain was a little annoyed that the pirate in red should have brought this up again.

'Aarrrr. This is definitely the place—see, Old Jack marked that the treasure was next to a shrub which looked like the rude part of a lady.' He pointed at the map and then at the shrub that was shaped just like a woman's bare ankle. A couple of the pirates giggled and nudged each other.

'I know it's hard work, me beauties, but it's going to be worth it!'

Much to the Pirate Captain's relief, before any further discussion could take place there came the unmistakable clank of spade against wood.

'Hooray!' yelled the sassy pirate. 'I found a treasure chest!'

With a new surge of energy, the crew hefted an antique chest up onto the sand.

'The ultimate treasure!' said the Pirate Captain, a little embarrassed to actually find himself salivating at the prospect. He wiped a big bit of slobber away with his sleeve. 'This is pay day, lads!' he added, after a suitably dramatic pause.

As the Pirate Captain forced the rusty hinges with his cutlass, the crew backed away a little just in case a mummy or a zombie pirate should jump out, because it wouldn't be the first time. But instead of a mummy or a zombie pirate there was just a solitary picture of a grinning child with a brief note scrawled on the back of it.

Isn't the ultimate treasure a child's smile? Isn't a drop of rain on the wing of a butterfly worth a million doubloons?
Yours, Calico Jack

'Oh,' said the Pirate Captain, biting his lip. 'Isn't that nice?'

Somewhere a parrot squawked.

'Yes,' said the pirate with a scarf, who looked like he was about to burst into tears. 'And it's so true. When you think about it.'

'We've learnt an important lesson today about what's really valuable,' said the pirate in green through clenched teeth.

The pirates spent the next few minutes avoiding each other's gaze and saying how this was much better than the ultimate treasure turning out to be something predictable like jewels or gold. Calico Jack's message so impressed the albino pirate that he kicked the head off one of the baby seals that were mucking about on the beach. The crew reluctantly picked up their spades and hats and trudged silently back to where the *Lovely Emma* was parked.

Eventually the Pirate Captain couldn't help himself. 'I'm not saying I'm not richer in spirit or anything,' he said, 'but it would have been nice if there'd been a bit of booty in there as well.'

The pirate crew all started talking at once.

'All that digging and not a single bloody diamond!'

'The wing of a butterfly? A *butterfly*?'

'Calico Spack, more like!'

Five

SATAN'S FISH ATE US ALIVE!

'Well, lads, you'll be happy to know I have a new plan,' said the Pirate Captain, striking his most businesslike pose. The pirate crew, who were all sprawled on one of the *Lovely Emma*'s tennis courts awaiting their Captain's idea, gazed up at him expectantly.

'We're going,' said the Pirate Captain, a glint in his eye, 'to Las Vegas!'

The pirates all looked at each other in surprise. It wasn't exactly the announcement they had been anticipating.

'Las Vegas?'

'That's right. Las Vegas. The city of dreaming spires.'

'But you're always saying how gambling is terrible, Pirate Captain. You said it was even worse than calling people names.'

'But then we had that adventure where you wagered the whole boat and crew that nobody could beat you at thumb-wrestling.'

'Which is it, Pirate Captain?' said the albino pirate. 'Is gambling terrible or good?'

'We are not,' said the Pirate Captain, 'going to Vegas to gamble.'

'Oh. Why *are* we going? Is it the whoring?'

'No, it's not that either. Come on, you lubbers—what else is Las Vegas famous for?'

The pirate crew gave a collective shrug.

'Showbusiness! You know how good I am at telling anecdotes. And we're always having adventures. It's just the sort of place an entertaining act such as ourselves could be a hit.'

The pirates wriggled uncomfortably from foot to foot. A couple of them tapped their heads meaningfully.

'Come on!' bellowed the Pirate Captain. 'It was bound to come down to this sooner or later. Why are you all looking so put out?'

'It's just . . . I don't think we realised you had ambitions in that particular direction,' said the pirate with a scarf.

'It's not just one of my fads, if that's what you mean.'

'Are you sure about this, Captain?' said the pirate in red.

'I do have a sensitive side, you know,' said the Pirate Captain with a pout. 'I realise you lot tend to think I'm just about the hair and the grisly murder, but that's simply not the case. You might be surprised to hear that sometimes I enjoy taking a little time out to read Shakespeare, and make daisy chains, and artistic stuff like that. I've always felt a certain calling for the stage. In many ways I think that's why I got into piracy in the first place, because it's quite dramatic.'

'Sorry, Captain,' said the pirate in green. 'I hope you haven't felt too misunderstood all these years.'

'Aaarrr, that's okay. It's a lonely job, being a Pirate Captain. I knew that when I signed on.'

The crew were pretty tired by the time the *Lovely Emma* arrived in Las Vegas[14], because even though this adventure was taking place in America, they still had to sail across Texas and half of Nevada. There

14 In 1829 Santa Fe merchant Antonio Armijo led a party on the Old Spanish Trail to Los Angeles. When they discovered an abundance of artesian water in a valley, they named it 'Las Vegas', Spanish for 'the Fertile Valley'.

was a hair-raising encounter along the way with a shoal of box jellyfish, which washed up onto the deck during a typhoon, and the Pirate Captain had to make sure the crew were all wearing their pirate shoes: 'Something you should do anyway,' he pointed out, 'because of verrucas.' The pirates had then spent an enjoyable afternoon running around the boat smacking the jellyfish with spades.

Luckily for the pirates the Las Vegas of those days was a lawless place, so just for once they didn't have to disguise themselves as washerwomen or scientists or anything like that to avoid getting arrested. In fact, life in the American Wild West was really a lot like life on the High Seas. Obviously there were a few minor differences, but these were pretty superficial—it was mostly a matter of certain things being known by different names. The pirate with a scarf gave out a list to the rest of the crew, just to avoid any confusion whilst they were there:

The High Seas		**The American Wild West**
Pirates	=	*Cowboys*
Walking the plank	=	*Lynchings*
Exotic Palm Trees	=	*Cacti*
Sharks	=	*Rattlesnakes*
Ham	=	*Jerky*
Roaring	=	*Whooping*
Shanties	=	*Campfire songs*
Lubbers	=	*Varmints*
Rip-roaring adventure	=	*Hornswoggling adventure*
Jellyfish	=	*Coyotes*

The crew all dutifully memorised their lists, parked the boat in a lake next to some cowboy wagons, and went to have a look about the place. The pirates were very excited by the Las Vegas buildings, which were in the shape of buildings that you wouldn't expect to find in the middle of the desert. The Pirate Captain tried to look nonchalant, because he didn't want to undermine the world-weary been-there-done-that image he liked to cultivate, but it wasn't easy because he was almost as excited as the men.

'Look at that one,' said the pirate in green. 'It's like a real medieval castle! Like we have in England!'

'That one's shaped like a pyramid!'

'And that one's shaped like a *pirate boat*!'

The pirates couldn't help but gawp at all the bright lights and the glamorous people walking down the strip. The prevalent fashion in Las Vegas appeared to be ten-gallon hats and handlebar moustaches for the men and 'almost bare' for the ladies.

The pirates all looked with big longing eyes at one of the glittering casinos. And then they all looked with big pleading eyes at their Captain. A few of them started to bounce up and down on the spot, which was always a sure sign that they were getting overexcited.

'Please, Pirate Captain!' said the pirate with rickets.

'*Please*,' said the pirate with gout.

'We could get one of those almost bare ladies to blow on our dice with real lady breath,' said the pirate in red.

'I heard it's impossible to lose when they do that!' said the pirate with a nut allergy.

'Snake eyes!' shouted the albino pirate. He wasn't sure what it meant, but he wanted to join in.

The Pirate Captain sighed. 'I suppose it wouldn't be the end of the world. And besides, let's not forget that last adventure we had in a casino,' he added, winking at his second-in-command. 'There's always the chance that some bored millionaire type will offer me a fortune to let him spend one night with the pirate with a scarf.'

The pirates headed straight for the roulette[15] table, because it had a big shiny spinning wheel on it, and just like magpies pirates tend to find themselves drawn to shiny things.[16]

15 Blackbeard is said to have invented a game he called 'Pirate Roulette'. When he was very bored he would lock himself in the hold with his crew and let off a volley of random shots with his pistol. Then he would count how many dead pirates there were.

16 Barracudas, sometimes known as the 'Tigers of the Sea', are also a lot like magpies, as they are attracted to shiny reflective things, which has led to a number of attacks on necklace-wearers.

The pirates tried to decide if it was best putting their doubloons on black or on red. Half of the pirates argued that it was best to put them on black, because that was the colour of their sturdy pirate boots. And the other half thought it was best to put them on red, because that was the colour of blood, and they wanted to show that they were a murderous bunch. In the end they compromised and put their doubloons on the little green zero, because that was the colour of rolling fields back in England, and they were all feeling a little homesick.

Ten minutes later, having lost not only the emergency doubloons taped to the bottom of the teapot but also the teapot itself, the pirates were starting to think that perhaps the Pirate Captain had been right in the first place, and that maybe gambling wasn't so great after all. They decided to go and play on the slot machines with their last few pieces of eight.

'I think it's obvious that table was rigged, Pirate Captain,' said the pirate in green.

'And I didn't like the look of that croupier. Did you notice that he had no ear lobes? I remember hearing that's a sure sign of dishonesty in a man,' said the pirate with gout.

'Don't be too disheartened, lads,' said the Pirate Captain. 'After all, you're forgetting the actual reason we're here. We've come to put on a show!' To illustrate the point he did a little tap-dance whilst holding an imaginary cane, and in the process accidentally bumped into an elderly man who was sat at one of the slot machines a little way along. The man let out a muffled curse, and his leg clattered onto the floor.

'Oh good grief! I've knocked your leg off! I'm so sorry!' said the Pirate Captain, stricken. 'I don't know my own strength sometimes.'

It was then he noticed that the leg which was lying on the floor wasn't a normal-looking leg, but a chunk of glinting whalebone. He looked up to see a scowling face with a livid scar that he recognised as belonging to the friendly stranger from Nantucket docks.

'Ahab! It is Ahab, isn't it?' said the Captain.

'Pirate Captain,' said Ahab.

The Pirate Captain handed Ahab his leg back.

'Thank you,' said Ahab, and then he rather joylessly turned back to the slot machine.

'Fancy seeing you here! I thought you were off looking for that whale.'

Ahab turned a sullen eye on the Captain. 'Aye, Pirate Captain. Ahab does not rest. Some of my whaler crew told me that the white fiend had been sighted here.'

'Really? Here in the desert? Not the usual habitat, is it?'

'He is a mighty devious beast, Captain.'

'I suppose he must be,' said the Pirate Captain thoughtfully.

'The men informed me that they had seen the whale entering into this very casino. Gambling is a filthy vice, as I'm sure you would agree, but one I find not in the least surprising from a creature so lacking in honest virtue.'

There was a sharp pinging sound from Ahab's slot machine, and a pile of shiny doubloons poured out onto the old whaler's lap. The Pirate Captain looked at them wistfully.

'Ahab seems to have got three lemons,' said Ahab. He scooped up his winnings and heaved a weary sigh. 'But what is money to me? Only cold revenge can soothe a soul such as mine.'

'Yes, cold revenge sounds good. Or maybe you should go and take in a show,' suggested the Pirate Captain with a hopeful grin. 'It just so happens that me and the lads here are planning on putting on a bit of a performance ourselves. I'm sure you'd enjoy it, and it may take your mind off the whaling for a while.'

'I am sorry, Captain. I have no time for such things,' said Ahab, screwing his whalebone leg back into place and getting up from his stool. 'And the beast appears to have given me the slip once more, so if you'll excuse me, Ahab must take his leave.'

And with a brisk nod of his well-weathered head, Ahab stalked out of the casino.

'Are all your friends that dour, Captain?' asked the pirate with a hook for a hand as the pirates wandered back to the *Lovely Emma*.

'Only the ones racked with eternal torment,' explained the Captain. 'The rest are pretty frivolous.'

The pirates quickly busied themselves making a little stage out of some barrels and planks of wood from the boat's lumber room. They used one of her sails to make a theatrical curtain and put out deckchairs at the front for the audience. Meanwhile the Pirate Captain locked himself up in his office with a broad selection of coloured pens, scissors, and glue. When he eventually came out he was looking pretty pleased with himself. He unfurled a huge banner:

THE PIRATE CAPTAIN PRESENTS:
A CAVALCADE OF CUTLASS CAPERS!

Featuring:

The PIRATE CAPTAIN recounting his best anecdotes (both nautical and land-based)!
Jennifer (an actual lady) throwing knifes!
The tallest pirate on the Seven Seas!
Pirates doing rousing shanties!
The PIRATE CAPTAIN's moving monologues!
An albino that walks like a man!
And divers other entertainments, culminating in the grand finale, where the PIRATE CAPTAIN will knock out a ferocious lion with a single punch!

'What do you think, lads?'

'I like the alliteration, Pirate Captain,' said the pirate with a scarf.

'Yes,' said the Pirate Captain proudly. 'I thought of doing it with Ks—you know, Kavalcade of Kutlass Kapers. But then I thought that might be a bit much.'

'I can see that,' said the pirate with a scarf. 'Are you really going to knock out a ferocious lion?'

'Not as such. Well, *no*. I might have been embellishing.'

After the pirates had hung the banner over the back of the *Lovely Emma* and had gone round the dusty little town handing out a few flyers, the Pirate Captain decided it was time to rehearse.

'Right, lads, let's get this show on the road! I thought we'd start by workshopping a few scenes—you know, to get a feel of our roles.'

'Erm . . . I was just going to do a couple of shanties, to be honest,' said the pirate in green. 'I was thinking educational for the matinee and a little more bawdy in the evening.'

'That sounds good,' said the Pirate Captain. 'What about you, Jennifer? How's the knife-throwing coming along?'

'Oh, I've not really tried it yet,' said Jennifer airily. 'But it can't be that hard, can it? It's only knifes after all. Just to be on the safe side, I thought I'd use the pirate with a peg-leg as my partner, seeing as he's already so used to losing bits and pieces.'

Jennifer smiled at the pirate with a peg-leg. The pirate with a peg-leg looked a bit miserable.

The pirate in green went round the audience with his hat to collect the night's takings. Just about all of Wild West life was there—millionaires, cowboys, native Americans, and even a few women of ill repute. He knew that the people in Vegas had a bit of a reputation, so when he was collecting the doubloons he bit down on them, because he had seen people do this before, but he wasn't sure why, because all he could tell was that it made his fillings hurt.

Behind the curtain the Pirate Captain was doing a few stretching exercises and going over his lines.

'Now. Do you think I should do the mosquito anecdote?'

'I should say the shark anecdote is better, Captain,' replied the scarf-wearing pirate.

'It occurred to me, as some sort of framing device, I might explain the story behind each of my scars.'

'That's a good idea, Captain.'

'This nasty one here? That's the time I had my BCG.'

'Yes, Captain. I remember the nurse said you were very brave.'

'I think the rest are all from slipping over in the bath.'

'The ocean certainly is a rocky mistress.'

The scarf-wearing pirate gave the sassy pirate a nod, the sassy pirate tugged on a rope and up went the makeshift curtain.

'Hello Las Vegas!' said the Pirate Captain, waving to the audience with both hands. 'It's lovely to be here!'

The show got off to an energetic start, with all the pirates doing a shanty about swimming really fast. Next up was the tallest pirate on the Seven Seas, who came on and did a little dance to the sound of an accordion. The tallest pirate on the Seven Seas was wearing a very long coat and had a normal-sized head that looked a lot like the pirate in green's head. When the tallest pirate on the Seven Seas left the stage to a polite round of applause he nearly fell over as his top half turned to bow to the audience and his bottom half continued into the wings.[17] Then there was some tumbling from some of the

17 The tallest man ever was Robert Wadlow, standing 8' 11" in his stockinged feet. He was medically a giant—a condition caused by an excess of growth hormone. Tall stature is accompanied by broad, spade-like fingers, overdeveloped jaw and cheekbones, and a disproportionately large skull.

more lively pirates and after that the Pirate Captain invited a few children up onto the stage. He magicked some eggs from behind their ears, sat them all on a bench and got them to sing a jolly shanty about the harsh life of a pirate. The Pirate Captain warned them that the theatre was haunted and that they had to keep singing—even if a scary ghost came and touched their shoulder. As the children sang, the albino pirate sneaked on and chased them off one by one, until only the littlest kid was left, absolutely terrified out of his wits, whilst the Pirate Captain chuckled away. Then the Pirate Captain told him that it was all okay and that the ghost was actually just an albino. He let the littlest kid feed the albino a couple of pieces of meringue to see how harmless he was. Then the Pirate Captain sang a shanty to the kid about how we have to look after the children, because they are our future. The show finished with the Pirate Captain's moving environmental monologue that he had entitled 'The Last Dolphin In The Sea'. It was a bit downbeat, because he had written it when he was in a mood and it had been raining, but the pirates all agreed that the environment was a serious matter and needed to be treated as such. Halfway through the monologue the accordion broke, but fortunately the pirate with asthma was on hand to step up and do 'human accordion', which was a bit like human beatbox, but with more emphasis on wheezing.

'. . . where are my friends,
Oh where can they be?
Life is so lonely when you're
The last dolphin in the sea!'

'Remember. There's magic inside each and every one of you. Never forget that,' said the Pirate Captain, wiping a tear from his cheek and bowing to the audience as the curtain came down. All the pirates were buzzing.

'That went brilliantly, Captain!' said the pirate with a scarf, clutching a big bag of the evening's takings. He'd drawn a big thermometer to show how close they were getting to the six thousand doubloons and he set about colouring in the current total.

'It did go well, didn't it?' said the Captain, dabbing at his forehead with a handkerchief. 'I think I was born to thc stage, lads. This is my calling. If you cut me, do I not bleed greasepaint?'

'I'm sure that during our adventure with a circus you said you had sawdust in your veins, Captain.'

'Aaarrr. Yes. Also greasepaint. Sawdust and greasepaint.'

'That must make a sort of gooey paste, Captain.'

Six

DEATH FEAST OF THE PANTHER WOMEN!

'. . . So I said to him, "Larry—you can't go on like that, you just *can't*!" '

The Pirate Captain was regaling the pirates with a theatrical anecdote.

'And do you know what? He bloody did! He went on and *bloody stormed it*. Great times, lads. Great times.'

The pirates all sighed and shook their heads at Larry. Since the night before, the Pirate Captain had become an even better raconteur than ever, with a ready supply of funny and moving tales from the wonderful world of showbusiness.

'Five-minute call, Mr Captain!' shouted the pirate with a strawberry birthmark, and the pirates started scurrying about for the second night's performance. The Pirate Captain took a moment to tease his eyebrows into points. He stopped to look approvingly at himself in a mirror.

'ME ME ME. MO MO MO. MA MA MA,' he said to his reflection. The pirate in green straightened his hat for him. 'They're pretty quiet out there, Captain,' said the pirate in green.

'I expect they're trembling in anticipation. They'll have been looking forward to it all day.'

The Pirate Captain closed his eyes, took a deep breath and bounded onto the stage.

'Laaaadies and Gentlemen! Live on stage, fresh from the Seven Seas, it is *I*, the Pirate Captain! Raarggh!'

He waited for the applause. And he waited. After a bit more waiting he opened his eyes. There was nobody there. Just row upon row of empty deckchairs.[18]

'You can come out,' said the Pirate Captain. 'I'm not really that terrifying!'

'I don't understand it, Captain,' said the pirate with a hook for a hand, as they wandered disconsolately down one of Las Vegas's brightly lit streets.

'The reviews felt you were a "powerhouse of performance",' said the pirate in green.

'Fame is fickle,' said the scarf-wearing pirate wisely.

The Pirate Captain shook his head. 'It doesn't make any sense, lads. Yesterday we were all the rage, and now we can't shift a single ticket. It's a mystery.'

He took out the pirate with a scarf's useful table from a pocket and grumpily doodled an extra couple of columns:

The High Seas (*pirates*)	**The Wild West (*cowboys*)**
Pushes theatrical boundaries	*Lack of artistic vision*
Brilliant hats	*Rubbish hats*

18 Deckchairs can be quite dangerous—the Portuguese dictator Antonio de Oliveira Salazar suffered a fatal heart attack after getting himself entangled in a deckchair.

He was just about to add a third column about how much better his removable shiny pirate boots were compared to the dirty old cowboy boots that cowboys couldn't take off when, with a *tap tap tapping* sound, who should they spot but Ahab hurrying down the dusty street.

'Hello Ahab,' the Pirate Captain called out. 'Any joy? Whale-wise, I mean?'

Ahab hobbled sternly towards them. 'Ill-fortune besets me as ever, Captain. The leviathan has eluded me once again—the men tell me he must have slipped out the back of the casino just as we arrived.'

'He's a tricky so-and-so, isn't he?' said the Pirate Captain. 'You wouldn't expect something that big to be so stealthy, would you? Considering he's got no legs.'

Ahab glowered. 'I could spend an afternoon telling you tales of the beast's monstrous cunning, Pirate Captain. But I have an appointment to keep, so I cannot stop and chit-chat.'

'Oh, off anywhere interesting?'

'I am visiting a theatre show.'

The pirates were a little put out by this. 'I thought you said you were too busy to go to see shows?' said the pirate with a scarf.

'Ahab is a solemn fellow,' said Ahab. 'I take no pleasure from playacting. But the men insisted that after the white whale left the casino, they spotted him buying tickets for a show. This, apparently, was his choice.'

Ahab handed the Pirate Captain a theatrical flyer. The Pirate Captain's beetling brows almost leapt off his face.

'Hell's teeth! The *rogue*!'

For there, printed in a gothic pirate script above a picture of a boat, they read:

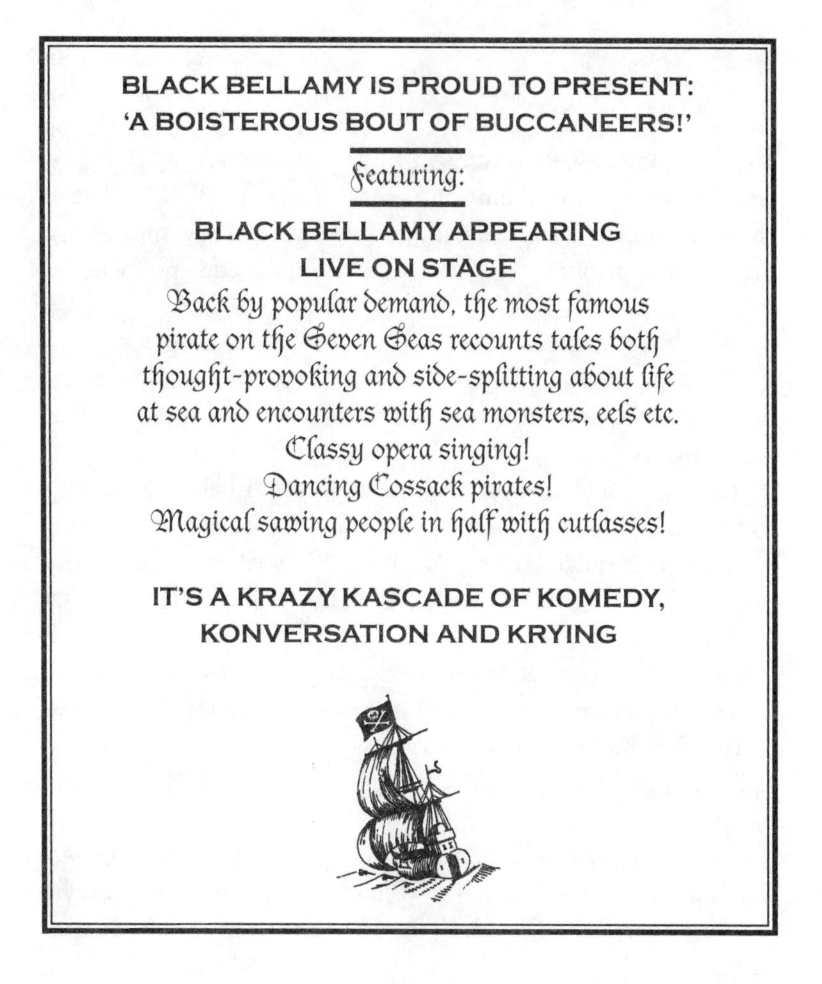

BLACK BELLAMY IS PROUD TO PRESENT:
'A BOISTEROUS BOUT OF BUCCANEERS!'
Featuring:
BLACK BELLAMY APPEARING LIVE ON STAGE
Back by popular demand, the most famous pirate on the Seven Seas recounts tales both thought-provoking and side-splitting about life at sea and encounters with sea monsters, eels etc.
Classy opera singing!
Dancing Cossack pirates!
Magical sawing people in half with cutlasses!
IT'S A KRAZY KASCADE OF KOMEDY, KONVERSATION AND KRYING

'So that's why nobody came to our show!' exclaimed the pirate in green.

'It's almost as if he does this sort of thing just to cause us mischief!' said the pirate in red.

'Whilst I have no time for such fripperies, one must admit that it's very clever how they've done all those Ks, do you not think, Pirate Captain?' said Ahab.

The Pirate Captain was so angry that he didn't even stop to buy popcorn before he, Ahab, and the pirates burst into Black Bellamy's show. Black Bellamy was already up on stage, halfway through taking questions about cuisine from a girl from the audience who was sat on his knee.

'What's the bounciest meat in the world?' asked the girl.

'Good question,' said Black Bellamy. 'There isn't actually a bounciest meat in the world, but the chewiest meat is beef jerky, which comes from dry cows.'

'I see no sign of the accursed sea-beast,' said Ahab, scanning the auditorium, 'but my godforsaken crew are obviously enjoying themselves,' he added bitterly, looking at his whalers sat in the front row. Ahab paused, and turned to the pirates. 'You might say that they are having a whale of a time.'

The pirates looked at Ahab. There was an embarrassed silence.

'That was a joke,' said Ahab. 'Whale of a time. You see?'

The pirates went on looking at Ahab.

'I rarely make jokes,' said Ahab, a little sadly. 'I don't really have the delivery.'

Black Bellamy had finished with his question-and-answer session, and now he had begun to recount a story about the time he had disguised himself as Admiral Nelson and sunk Napoleon's flagship.

'It's funny, it's moving, and it's educational,' whispered one of the audience to their neighbour.

'Much better than that other pirate last night. Much classier.'

'And I like the way his beard goes right up to his eyes.'

The Pirate Captain was just about to tap the fellow on the shoulder and point out that Black Bellamy was just an old ham, by which he certainly did not mean the good kind of mouth-watering old ham, when there was another wild round of applause.

'Thank you very much, ladies and gentlemen,' said Black Bellamy, waving for them to calm down. 'I'm now going to sing you a shanty that is very close to my heart. As you know, I care a great deal about the environment . . . This one is called "The Last Dolphin In The Sea".'

'Oh, honestly!' cried the Pirate Captain. 'That really is the final straw! Excuse me, Ahab.' And with that the Pirate Captain charged up through the audience and onto the stage.

'Hello Pirate Captain,' said Black Bellamy in a laconic voice. 'Fancy seeing you here.'

'Don't you "hello" me,' said the Pirate Captain, waggling his cutlass. 'You're stealing my material, you cove!'

'Pirate Captain! I don't even know how to begin to respond to such a baseless accusation.'

The Pirate Captain drew himself up to his full height of five feet and nine inches. 'I've had enough, you swab. We're going to settle this in the time-honoured pirate fashion!'

'Cutlasses?' shouted a helpful audience member.

'Pistols maybe?' shouted another excitedly.

'Wrestling naked in front of a roaring log fire?'

'Is it something to do with eating?'

'No,' said the Pirate Captain, turning to the audience. 'We're going to have a shanty battle. *Mano-a-mano*, with only our voices and ready wit as weapons! What do you say, Black Bellamy?'

'Why not?' roared Black Bellamy.

The audience cheered as the pirate with the accordion began to play a simple hornpipe. The Pirate Captain tapped his foot a few times.

'Walking with my big pirate boots on the deck,
Here comes the Pirate Captain with my broad neck,
I sing with confidence, finesse, and flair,
My clothes are the best and so is my hair!'

The crew and audience joined in on a chorus of 'Yo ho hos' and the Pirate Captain fixed Black Bellamy with a challenging eye. Black Bellamy swaggered confidently to the front of the stage.

'When admirals cry into their pillows at night,
It's Black Bellamy who caused their terrible plight!
I've plundered all of the Seven Seas and more,
Get out of my way when you hear me roar!'

As the crowd sang the chorus, Black Bellamy did a special backwards walk that looked as if his feet were walking forwards. The Pirate Captain stepped up.

'I move across the stage with sinuous grace,
Singing all the while from my pleasant, open face,
This Black Bellamy's show is a useless waste,
And if you think otherwise then you have no taste!'

On the last line, the Pirate Captain pointed an accusing finger at the audience and was met with a chorus of markedly less enthusiastic yo ho hos.

'The only thing more famous than my piratical crimes,
Is the super quality of my amazing rhymes
You try your hardest, but your shanties are jokes,
And then you insult these stand-up folks!'

Black Bellamy gestured to the crowd, who nodded and glared at the Pirate Captain. The Pirate Captain puffed out his chest.

'Only idiots couldn't see that you're a fraud.
I should have expected this from people abroad!
They're vulgar and crass and . . .'

'I don't think they appreciated you saying that about their mothers, Captain,' said the pirate with a scarf as they sprinted down the street a few minutes later.

'You may be right, Number Two,' said the Pirate Captain, using his cutlass to knock aside a bottle that was aimed at his head.

'It's been a while since we've had an angry mob after us, hasn't it, Captain?' said the pirate in green.

'Not since the adventure with the Catholic girls' school!' said the pirate with long legs.

'I feel a bit bad about Ahab.'

'You mean his leg snapping off? I'm sure he's got lots of spares.'

'Yes, I suppose being trampled by furious cowboys would be nothing compared to having your leg bitten off by a whale.'

'I've decided that showbusiness isn't really for me,' said the Pirate Captain, trying to remember where they had left the boat.

'It's a bit shallow, Captain,' agreed the pirate with a hook for a hand.

'Exactly,' said the Pirate Captain. 'The public aren't really ready for my material. It may be that I'm one of those innovative types who are doomed to only be appreciated by future generations.'

Seven

AT THE COURT OF THE CRABS!

Next morning, after a terrible dream involving Cutlass Liz and his beard and a big pair of rusty scissors, the Pirate Captain woke to the sound of bits of pirate bones trickling through the egg-timer. He tramped bleary-eyed into the boat's breakfast room. Usually he would have expected to find it full of the merry sounds of pirates staging little naval battles, with their cornflakes as tiny galleons and the milk as the sea, and the sizzle of bacon as distant cannon fire, but today he was greeted only by a restrained munching.

'Ka-boom!' said the Pirate Captain, as he sat down and spooned some cereal into his mouth, pretending it was Royal Navy boats and that his mouth was a big whirlpool.

'Hooray! Take that Royal Navy!' a couple of the crew replied, but more than a little halfheartedly.

The Pirate Captain scratched glumly at his bushy eyebrows. 'Number Two,' he said to the pirate with a scarf. 'As soon as these breakfast things have been cleared away, I want us to make sail for Nantucket.'

'What about the six thousand doubloons?' asked the albino pirate, not able to look the Captain in the eye.[19]

'Aaarrr,' said the Pirate Captain. 'We just have to face it, lads—I'm not going to be able to raise the cash in time. I've given it my best shot. We're going to have to hand back the boat.' The men stared at their plates. 'Besides, there's always a chance Cutlass Liz will decide that a stern telling-off would be a lot less bother than all that messy murdering,' the Captain added unconvincingly.

'Can't give up now, sir,' said the pirate with rickets. A few of the pirates whispered to each other and then the albino pirate held up a little bag.

'We've had a bit of a whip-round, Captain,' he said, passing it rather shyly across the table. The Pirate Captain tipped the bag out next to his plate. It contained:

- *3 pieces of eight*
- *Some foreign coins*
- *A chocolate groat with fluff on it*
- *A 'one child gets in free' voucher to see the lunatics at Bedlam*
- *An apple core*

'Oh . . .' The Captain pushed the contents about with his fork. 'Is that it?'

'Those foreign coins could be valuable,' said the pirate in green hopefully.

'This one's from Water-flumeland,' said the Pirate Captain, holding it up to the light, 'which I don't think is even a real country.'

'We tried our best!' said the pirate with rickets, distraught.

'I know you did,' said the Pirate Captain. 'And I'm touched, really I am. But we're in a pickle. We've tried treasure maps and showbusiness, and you've already said you don't much care for me pulling the gold teeth from every man here. So if you know any

19 This is as a result of the embarrassment of the situation, not because the Pirate Captain is too bright and shiny for the albino pirate's sensitive eyes.

other way a pirate can come by a bit of loot, I'd certainly like to hear it.'

'Why don't you become the spokesperson for treasure?' said the sassy pirate. 'My uncle was the spokesperson for Beecham's Pills, and he got a lifetime's supply of them for free. You should do that, but for gold and jewels and that kind of thing—I'm sure they'd like to be associated with you.'

'Or we could start making shell animals, to sell as souvenirs. Everybody likes shell animals, and we have ready access to plenty of shells.'

'Or we could,' said the pirate in red, rolling his eyes, 'try some pirating.'

'Eh?'

'You know—attacking boats and making off with their treasure. What with us being pirates and all.'

Even though the Pirate Captain didn't care much for the pirate in red's tone, he had to admit that the idea had a certain logic. Now the pirate in red had pointed it out, the Pirate Captain wasn't really sure why it hadn't occurred to them earlier. So after they had finished their breakfast and drunk some coffee, the noisy pirate climbed up to the crow's nest[20] to look out for passing boats to plunder, whilst the rest of the crew got busy, polishing the cannons and swabbing the decks. They hoisted the Jolly Roger, to show they were back in business, but some of the younger pirates felt the skeleton face was a little too frightening, so they took it back down and used a flag that showed the Pirate Captain waving instead. The Pirate Captain himself took up his position at the ship's wheel and rested his hat on a barrel in order to let his glossy hair and beard billow in the wind. He was just thinking how he might get a portrait commissioned in exactly this pose when they spotted their first boat.

Pirating being a lot like riding a bicycle or making out with a pretty girl, the basics soon came back to them. They braced the

20 Early sailors used actual crows to help with navigation, which were kept in cages at the top of the main mast. A released crow would inevitably head for land, allowing the ship's navigator to plot a course. If it didn't find land, the crow presumably just fell into the sea and died.

mainsail and fired the cannons and fixed their faces into terrible grimaces, did all the usual roaring and generally made for a fairly horrific sight.[21] The pirates were slightly disappointed that the boat turned out to be a leper ship. The lepers were really very understanding, and the pirates came away with some nice bells and a hefty stack of old leper parts, which they thought they might be able to sell to hospitals later on. [22] The second boat they attacked was full of children out on a school trip. The pirates made a few doubloons by selling the children some opium, and they all had a great time together building Frankensteins out of the bits of leper they had just collected. When it was time to go home several of the children asked if they could maybe stay and be pirates too, but the Pirate Captain was adamant that they should get back to their mothers, who would be worrying about where they were.

The pirate with a scarf picked up a telescope—making sure to check the eyepiece first, because on board the pirate boat the general consensus seemed to be that 'the old gags were the best'—and scanned the horizon.

'Ship ahoy, Captain.'

'Well, third time lucky,' said the Pirate Captain, a little wearily. 'It's definitely not penniless refugees or a ghost ship or something like that?'

'Can't quite tell, Captain. Bit small. Well weathered, but somehow . . . I don't know . . . almost *noble.* And she's covered with ivory, by the looks of it.'

'That sounds more like it. Ivory. White gold! Remember our adventure with elephants?'

21 When he wasn't inventing games, Blackbeard used to have hemp wicks coated with saltpetre attached to his hat, which when lit would envelop his face in a cloud of smoke to make himself look demonic. He was also famed for belching loudly to intimidate his victims.

22 There are two forms of leprosy, tuberculoid (dry) and lepromatous (wet). The former is characterised by death of nerves and is less contagious. In advanced cases, the latter can result in leontiasis which makes the victim's face look like a lion.

'Does it have a name?' said Jennifer, biting excitedly on a cutlass blade.

'The *Pequod.*'

'Funny sort of name for a boat.'

'Pirate Captain!' cried the albino pirate, and he came hurrying up, all out of breath and anxious-looking. 'We haven't got any cannonballs! We used them all up on the lepers and the school kids.'

'Honestly!' roared the Pirate Captain, 'what sort of an outfit are we running here? How can we not have any cannonballs?'[23]

'Well, we haven't got much of anything.'

The Pirate Captain had the scarf-wearing pirate bring up the inventory to conduct a quick recap:

20 limes
1 Prize Ham
2 dry cured hams
3 barrels of tar
1 pirate with an accordion (deceased and subsequently electroplated)

'We've finished all the biscuits?' asked the Captain in dismay.

'I'm afraid so, Captain.'

'We could fire a lime, sir,' suggested the pirate with a scarf. 'They're sort of the right shape.'

'Aaaarrr. Fair enough,' said the Pirate Captain. 'But dip it in tar so they think it's a cannonball. Otherwise we risk looking stupid.'

---

23 Cannons of the time required round iron cannonballs. It was important to store the cannonballs so that they could be of instant use when needed, yet not roll around the gun deck. The solution was to stack them up in a square-based pyramid next to the cannon. The top level of the stack had one ball, the next level down had four, the next had nine, the next had sixteen, and so on. The only real problem was how to keep the bottom level from sliding out from under the weight of the higher levels. To do this, they devised a small brass plate ('brass monkey') with one rounded indentation for each cannonball in the bottom layer. Brass was used because the cannonballs wouldn't rust to it as they would to an iron one. When temperature falls, brass contracts in size faster than iron. So as it got cold on the gun decks, the indentations in the brass monkey would get smaller than the iron cannonballs they were holding. If the temperature got cold enough, the bottom layer would pop out of the indentations, spilling the entire pyramid over the deck. Hence the expression 'cold enough to freeze the balls off a brass monkey'.

'Can we wear those dinosaur masks we picked up at the Natural History Museum on our last adventure?' asked the pirate who was always getting nosebleeds. 'I really think they add to our ferociousness.'

'Why not?' roared the Pirate Captain. 'You know I'm always encouraging you lot to improvise. Express yourselves! Above all else remember that it's meant to be fun—that's the secret of good pirating.'

So the pirates fired the *Lovely Emma*'s cannons a couple of times and drew up alongside the *Pequod*. The Pirate Captain grabbed hold of a hefty rope, swung across to the other boat—showing considerable athleticism, and not a little leg—and landed square in the middle of its deck. One of the *Pequod*'s men charged forward waving a dangerous-looking harpoon, but the Pirate Captain hacked at him with his cutlass and the man dropped to the deck, split right down the middle. Seeing this grisly spectacle, the rest of the *Pequod*'s crew backed off a bit, and the Pirate Captain was left face-to-face with a single brave soul.

'I'm the Pirate Captain!' said the Pirate Captain, twirling his cutlass like a baton in a move he had been up practising all the previous night. 'And I'm here for the loot!'

The man made no reply, but somehow his silence was fearsome in itself. A horrible sense of familiarity settled over the Pirate Captain. He squinted again at the fellow, and at his mop of straggly grey hair, and at the ugly scar that ran the length of one of his cheeks, and at the ivory leg poking out from the bottom of his trousers, and began to realise the terrible awkwardness of his situation.

'Oh dear,' said the Pirate Captain, turning a bright red.

Eight

DAMN YOU I SAY, DR. CHESINGTON!

In piratical circles this sort of thing was social death. For a moment the Pirate Captain thought about trying to pretend that he and the crew were some sort of pirate-a-gram, sent by one of Ahab's whaler mates. But whalers were a notoriously humourless lot, and it didn't seem likely they would have instigated such a thing.

'How incredibly embarrassing,' stuttered the Captain, grinning a weak grin. 'What are the odds? I mean, all the traffic cluttering up the shipping lanes nowadays, and I should run into you . . .'

The Pirate Captain trailed off. Ahab still hadn't said anything, but he seemed ready to explode. An angry-looking nerve had started to twitch in the corner of his eye. The Pirate Captain looked at his shoes. 'Sorry about running through, erm . . .'

'Mister Starbuck,' said Ahab icily.

'Yes. Sorry about running Mister Starbuck through. Do you think he'll be okay?'

'You've cleaved him clean in two.'

'I sort of have, haven't I? I bet I couldn't manage that again if I tried a thousand times! I—uh—hope that cannonball didn't do too much damage.'

'It wasn't a cannonball. It was a lime.'

'Yes. Well. Sorry anyway.'

'I have citric acid in my eye.'

'Oh. That must sting.'

'It does.'

The Pirate Captain awkwardly put away his cutlass, and waved for his pirate crew to stop their pirating. It was always nice to run into old acquaintances again, but this did pretty much scupper the whole operation. After all, there was a certain set of piratical ethics to be adhered to, and not stealing from a man who had offered you grog was just about at the top of the list.[24]

To try and make amends, the Pirate Captain invited Ahab and his crew to a meal on board the *Lovely Emma*. Usually the Pirate Captain wasn't much for having people to dinner, because it just meant less food for the pirates, but it seemed the least he could do, and he was actually quite pleased he had a guest to show off the new boat to.

'I like your *Pequod*,' said the Pirate Captain. 'Especially what you've done with all that whalebone about the place. I'm afraid that I'm not as creative as yourself, so all the fittings on board the *Lovely Emma* are just solid silver. I think the sails are made from chinchilla skin. And the ropes are all woven from the hair of only the best-looking women actresses.'

'She seems a sturdy vessel, Pirate Captain,' agreed Ahab grudgingly.

'We even have a dance studio. I only found that yesterday. Does the *Pequod* have a dance studio on board?'

'No, Pirate Captain, it does not. I do not approve of dance.'

'That's a pity. How about cup holders? Does the *Pequod* have any cup holders? Because the *Lovely Emma* has them all over the ship. No need to ever spill a drop of grog.'

24 Pirates were not entirely amoral. The otherwise bloodthirsty Bartholemew Roberts couldn't bring himself to kill a priest, even when he refused to become the pirate's chaplain. So he let the man go, but only after stealing two prayer books and a corkscrew from him.

'I do not approve of grog on board ship, Pirate Captain.'

'Aaarrrr,' said the Pirate Captain, who was beginning to think that Ahab wasn't turning out to be the best dinner guest in the world. 'I hope you haven't got anything against chops?' he added, as a big pile of chops was carried to the table by a couple of the pirate crew. The pirates and the whalers started to eat in awkward silence.

'So, Ahab,' said the Pirate Captain, trying to get the conversation going. 'Any luck finding that whale?'

Ahab's stony face seemed to set even harder.

'No, Pirate Captain. The beast has continued to evade me these past few days. Just last night I thought I'd finally cornered him, but it turned out to be a big bit of kelp.'

'I'm sure it's an easy mistake to make,' said the Pirate Captain sympathetically. 'It sounds a lot like the time I got into all that confusion with a mermaid.'

'A mermaid?' repeated Ahab, actually raising an eyebrow, though the rest of his face remained as impassive as ever.

'Oh yes. I went out with this charming mermaid for . . . oooh, how long would you say it was, Number Two?'

'About three months, Captain,' said the pirate with a scarf, looking a little pained.

'Yes, about three months. It took that long for the lads to convince me that it wasn't really a mermaid at all. It was just a regular fish.'

'Surely,' said Ahab, 'it is an easy enough distinction to make?'

'You would have thought that,' agreed the Captain, 'but what you have to appreciate is that the top half of that fish was just really very attractive. Normally I prefer the top halves of ladies to have arms and hair and all that, but this girl—or marlin, as I later came to realise—really carried it off. And she was a fantastic kisser.'

Ahab looked unimpressed. The Pirate Captain wondered if he should bring up the time they had sailed through an electrical storm and he had become magnetised, but somehow he felt Ahab wouldn't approve of that either.

'So, tell us all about whales then, Ahab,' said Jennifer eagerly.

'They're disgusting creatures,' said Ahab. 'Entirely without redeeming qualities.'

'But valuable, eh? You must make a packet from hunting them?'

'No, young lady. They're worthless. The "vermin of the sea". That's what I call them. And the white whale is the worst of the lot.'

'So why do you bother with them?'

'I hate them. I hate their small eyes, and I hate their wide mouths,' said Ahab, getting so annoyed his knuckles began to turn white.

'I'm a lot like that with mimes,' said the Captain with a nod. 'Can't bear them. All that pretending to get out of invisible boxes. Nonsense.'

'Whales are worse,' snarled Ahab. He viciously speared a piece of meat and chewed it with grim determination.

The other pirates were doing their best to make conversation with the whaler crew, but they were a strange bunch, and most of their stories placed a lot more emphasis on icebergs and interminable months spent at sea rather than feasts and fighting. Also, just as one of the whalers would actually seem to be getting to the point of an anecdote, they were liable to wander off suddenly on long and rather dull tangents about whale anatomy or things like that. The pirate in red was more than a little relieved when his conversation with a funny-looking whaler with one tooth and a lot of tattoos was interrupted by the booming voice of the Captain.

'Oho! What's this?' said the Pirate Captain, fighting back a grin. 'I do believe . . . Oh my! Why if I'm not mistaken . . . it's the WHITE WHALE ITSELF!'

Ahab started out of his chair. Several of the whalers reached for their harpoons. Then through the door to the kitchen came the pirate with a scarf and the pirate with gout, carrying a huge plate on which there sat a great pile of mashed potato. The mashed potato had been moulded roughly into the shape of a whale. It had radishes for eyes. The whalers put down their harpoons and settled grumblingly back into their seats.

'Are you mocking me, sir?' asked Ahab with a steely stare.

'Goodness! No! Not at all,' said the Pirate Captain defensively. 'It's just—look, it's made from mashed potato.' He spooned a dollop of potato from the whale's flank. 'See? We thought it would be a nice surprise,' he added sadly.

Ahab exhaled. 'I apologise. The truth is I'm tired, Pirate Captain. Tired of the ocean, and of this chase. In fact, we were heading back to Nantucket when you attacked.'

'Oh dear,' said the Pirate Captain. 'You mean to say you've given up? You're just going to let that whale mess about in the sea, splashing around and biting bits off of people?'

Ahab stood up and tapped the table with his whalebone foot until he had everybody's attention. His baleful eyes swept the room and seemed to look deep into the souls of every man there.

'Hold!' he shouted. 'Before you stands Ahab, a man. For the past age I have abandoned my humanity in pursuit of the demon that ate my leg. I have stared at raging seas, through storm and rain, until moss grew upon my clothes and icicles hung from my ears and nose. Aye! I have not relented. The bulldog which grips on until death—that has been Ahab. The sun which beats on the desert without reprieve—that has been Ahab. The stubborn stain which soap will not shift—that has been Ahab. The Vale of Death holds no horrors for me, for I seek only vengeance, which I shall pursue even after I lie beneath the mould of the grave.'

The Pirate Captain was about to suggest that perhaps Ahab might want to think about developing some other hobbies outside whaling, but the old whaler had not quite finished.

'My destiny is fixed—I shall be avenged. But of late I have grown weary and my stomach queasy when we hit choppy waters. Also, this is my last spare whalebone leg and if he snaps this one, Ahab is stuffed. So!' Ahab paused and did his looking-into-souls-with-his-eyes trick again. 'I have decided to put a price on the whale's accursed head and return to Nantucket.'

The whalers gasped and not a few of them looked absolutely delighted. Ahab produced a sheaf of leaflets which he handed to the Pirate Captain.

'Take one and pass them on, Captain. And read it—read it well. For I offer a reward of six thousand doubloons to the man who brings me the white whale.'

The pirates looked at the leaflets, which showed the details of the reward above a picture of a whale chomping on a leg.

'SIX THOUSAND DOUBLOONS!' shouted Ahab, to emphasise the point. Then he sat down and tucked into his fruit medley.

'That's a big reward,' remarked the Pirate Captain, 'for catching a fish.'

Ahab shrugged. 'I told you. I really, *really* don't get on with him.'

Nine

I RIDE WITH THE BANDIT KING!

After a game of chess that the Pirate Captain later told the pirates he deliberately let Ahab win because he still felt guilty about Mister Starbuck, they waved the crew of the *Pequod* goodbye. The Captain ordered all the pirates into one of the *Lovely Emma*'s spacious meeting rooms, where they sat trying to look studious as he wrote some things down on a blackboard. It wasn't easy, because keeping quiet and sitting still were not traits at which pirates tended to excel. The Pirate Captain wrote down TREASURE HUNTING in capital letters and then he crossed it through. Then he wrote SHOWBUSINESS and he crossed that out too, but with a bit more venom this time so that the chalk snapped off and hit the octagon-faced pirate in the eye. After that he wrote ACTUAL PIRATING and he crossed that out as well. Finally he wrote down WHALING and instead of crossing it out he drew a little tick and a smiley face next to it.

'I hope that makes everything clear,' said the Pirate Captain.

The crew muttered to each other, and the pirate in red put his hand up.

'I'm not saying it isn't a good idea, Pirate Captain,' he said. 'But you haven't really explained how we actually do it. The whaling, that is.'

'Oh, you know. Track the whale down, and bop him on the head.'

'Bop him on the head?'

The Pirate Captain mimed bopping the whale on the head. 'Bop. That's right. Something like that.'

'But how do we *find* the whale?' persisted the pirate in red, folding his arms and frowning to convey as much surliness as he dared.

The Pirate Captain looked stumped. His experience of this kind of thing was pretty limited. He had won a sizeable goldfish on Brighton Pier once, but that had involved throwing brightly coloured balls at coconuts, and he didn't really think that would do the trick in this case.

'Aarrr,' he said, drawing a few wavy lines on the blackboard and trying to sound knowledgeable. 'It's basically just a question of luring the whale onto your boat.'

'With magnets?' asked the sassy pirate.

'No. Not with magnets. I know you lot tend to think everything can be solved with magnets, but that's just not the case.'[25]

'What then?'

'Bait. We need to put out some whale bait.'

He wrote 'BAIT' on the blackboard and tapped it with his cutlass.

'What do we use for whale bait?' said the pirate with a hook for a hand.

'Whatever it is that whales like to eat.'

'Ooh! I know this!' said the pirate in green, waving his hand in the air. 'The answer's plankton. P-L-A-N-K-T-O-N.'

'You useless lubber!' roared the Pirate Captain. 'That's what they get to eat all the time. We need something that whales like *better* than plankton.'

'Ham?' suggested the pirate with rickets.

The Pirate Captain ran a hand through his luxuriant beard. He couldn't imagine a single creature, marine or otherwise, that wouldn't like ham. But they only had two regular hams left, and he didn't think

25 In fact, it is suspected that whales use the magnetic field of the Earth for navigation during their long migrations across the oceans. Many mass whale beachings occur at places where there is in an anomaly in the Earth's magnetic field.

he could bear to be parted from either of them. And he would sooner cut off his own stentorian nose than dangle his prize ham into the sea, only for some sea-beast to slobber all over it.

'You have to remember that this is no ordinary whale,' he said authoritatively. 'It's a white whale. And whales aren't normally white, are they? So it makes sense to suppose that it turned white by eating albinos. We'll start off by dangling the albino pirate over the side of the boat for a few days.'

The albino pirate seemed a little nonplussed by this idea. The other pirates cheered and slapped him on the back.

'I don't know what the rest of you are looking so smug about,' said the Pirate Captain. 'Just in case my albino theory is wrong—because believe it or not, I am wrong very occasionally—I want to see you lot swimming behind the boat, disguised as krill. Gigantic, fat, delicious krill.[26] That's sure to whet his appetite.'

The crew let out a collective groan that the Captain cut dead with his best withering look.

'Pirate Captain?' the pirate in red asked again. 'Is it really necessary for your plans to always involve us dressing up as something? Because some might say it borders on an unhealthy obsession.'

'Last time I checked, krill are tiny bioluminescent shrimp-like organisms that don't give backchat,' said the Pirate Captain with a sniff and a glower.

'Will *you* be dressing up as whale bait, Captain?'

'Obviously I'd love to,' said the Pirate Captain, rubbing the blackboard clean. 'But all that briny water could play havoc with my luxuriant beard. I'd hate to upset our large gay following, specifically those whose term for a hirsute gentleman such as myself is "a bear". Can't mess with the power of the pink pound! And it would be a shame not to share a nomenclature with such a fine animal.'

---

26 *Meganyctiphanes norvegica* form the base of many food chains around the world. Krill migrate daily, spending the daylight hours in deep waters and coming to the surface to feed and lay eggs at night.

Some of the pirates looked unconvinced by the Pirate Captain's logic.

'There is also a chance we get our pirating powers from my beard, like Samson did in that book. So there's another reason why I can't help.'

'Try to look more tasty!' the pirate with long legs shouted to the albino pirate.

The albino pirate's head resurfaced and he spat out a mouthful of seawater. 'I don't think this is really working. I've been nibbled by crabs and licked by a shark, but there's no sign of any whales!'

'You've only been in there an hour,' said the pirate in green.

'I can't feel my arms or legs!'

'How's it going, Number Two?' said the Pirate Captain, relaxing in the *Lovely Emma*'s deck-side paddling pool. He was reading a book about whales.

'We lost another cabin boy,' said the scarf-wearing pirate.

'Not the funny little one with the old man's face?' said the Pirate Captain, almost dropping his book.

'I'm afraid so, Pirate Captain. A barracuda ate him.'

'Good grief! Poor cabin boy. So young!'

'But with an old man's face,' said the pirate with a scarf wistfully.

'Yes. That's what gave him such character. Our adventures won't be the same without him.'

'And we've also lost quite a few krill-pirates to sharks and drowning,' added the pirate with a scarf.

'A funny thing about that,' said the Pirate Captain, nodding at his book about whales. 'It turns out that my research might not have been quite up to scratch. Apparently sperm whales don't eat krill at all. They're actually quite fussy eaters. Around eighty per cent of their diet is squids.'

This caused some grumbling from a few of the bedraggled krill-pirates swimming behind the boat. The Captain waved and shot them a guilty grin.

'Not to worry, lads. That isn't the only thing I've learnt. This is why I'm always trying to encourage you lot to read more, because you can discover some fascinating things from books. It says here that whales, despite their brutish appearance, are in fact famed for being the most sensitive and romantic creatures in the animal kingdom, not only tending to mate for life but also able to communicate with each other over distances of thousands of miles.'

'That's sweet, Captain, but I'm not sure I see how it helps us,' said the scarf-wearing pirate.

The Pirate Captain looked serious. 'It so happens, Number Two, that a love of the theatre has not been the only outlet for the more poetic aspects of my soul. You know all those times I've disappeared into my cabin and not allowed anybody to disturb me? It will come as a shock for you to learn that I've not really been studying my nautical almanacs as I may have previously led you to believe.'

'To be honest, Captain,' said the pirate in red, 'we always suspected that you might have been looking at that book of saucy etchings you keep on the top of your wardrobe.'

'Well I've not been doing that either, not that I have a clue what you're talking about. The fact is, these past few months I have been writing a *novel*. It's a romance.'

And somewhat sheepishly the Captain produced a manuscript from under his hat.

'I'm aware that this kind of thing is slightly frowned upon by the pirating fraternity, so obviously I will be using a pen name, should the frankly narrow-minded publishing industry ever choose to recognise my talents.'

The pirate crew breathed a quiet sigh of relief, because they could imagine what the Pirate King would have to say if he ever got wind of this.

'So what's the plan, Captain?'

'We'll simply do that trick of tying a couple of tin cans together with a piece of string,' explained the Pirate Captain, 'and then dangle one of the cans into the ocean so that the white whale is able to hear me read my novel aloud. Obviously I will do different voices for the various characters. It will be a lot like that business with Theseus and those Sirens—because of his sensitive soul the white whale will find himself drawn irresistibly towards us, and just as he's finding his huge baleen heart touched to the very core by my meditations on love and fate, bang! We harpoon him through the brain.'

The pirates almost all agreed that this sounded like a pretty foolproof plan.

'I'm very impressed, Captain,' said the pirate with a scarf. 'I didn't think you had it in you to write an entire novel. It's quite an achievement.'

'Oh, well, it's only about thirty-one thousand words,' said the Pirate Captain modestly. 'Bit cheeky to call it a novel really.'

The pirates fixed up the cans and string and then gathered around as the Pirate Captain made himself comfortable on a barrel. He cricked his neck and cleared his throat.

'*The Pirate Of My Heart*,' he began to read. 'Chapter One: "Love Across a Moonlit Sea".'

'Emerald was a proud, independent woman, fiery red locks of hair tumbling about her alabaster shoulders. She was free from that arrogant buccaneer, and she knew that fact should bring her only joy. But she could not help but think of his last words to her, those mischievous glittering eyes, and that firm, magnificent beard.

' "Emerald," he had said, "you are a treasure! Just like a real emerald! But you are an Irish princess, and I am a Pirate Captain! One day I shall make you mine, but for now I must go, and plunder the Spanish Main . . ."

'. . . Emerald looked under her pillow, and there she found a single white rose, as well as a battered old eye-patch. So perhaps it hadn't been a dream after all.'

The Pirate Captain closed his book and all the pirates clapped. But even though Emerald had made the right decision to follow her feelings and not marry the swarthy Spanish Duke, there was still no sign of the whale.

'Not to worry, Pirate Captain,' said the pirate in green. 'It must be that whales are not so clever and sensitive as people make out. Because your story was very good.'

'Yes,' agreed the pirate with long legs. 'I especially liked the way Emerald learned that the best way to get somebody to like you is simply to be yourself. Though of course it helps when yourself is a beautiful princess.'

'You enjoyed it then?' asked the Pirate Captain. 'Be honest though, because I really do value your opinions.'

The pirate in red looked as if he was about to say something, but the Captain hadn't quite finished. 'When I say "honest opinion" I'd like you to bear two things in mind. One—I don't take criticism particularly well at all, even the constructive kind. And two—I'm the Captain of this boat and I have an extremely sharp cutlass.'

The pirates' next plan was slightly less sensitive. 'I once saw a man doing this in the Thames,' explained the Pirate Captain with a wink to his second-in-command, as a couple of the pirates rolled a barrel of gunpowder off the side of the boat into the sea.

There was a muffled explosion, and then a few dead fish floated up to the surface. The Pirate Captain looked a little put out. 'But seeing as this is the ocean, which is a little bigger than the Thames, we might need a bit more gunpowder. Fetch us another couple of barrels, Number Two.'

A plume of water splashed across the deck and a shower of fish and lobsters crashed down onto the pirates' heads. The pirates looked about hopefully, but all they could see was a dying shark draped over the yardarm looking disappointedly back at them. 'No whales there,' said the pirate with a hook for a hand. They rolled a few more barrels off the side of the boat. Another huge wave crashed over the pirates, drenching them from head to toe, and another burst of creatures and seaweed rained onto the deck. The pirates prodded about in the mess.

'Still can't see him,' said the pirate in green, a bit of tentacle wriggling limply on his hat.

Jennifer pulled a starfish out of her top. 'It's fun though, isn't it?'

After the pirates ran out of barrels of gunpowder, the Pirate Captain had the bright idea of emptying all the *Lovely Emma*'s lamps and pouring the oil out from the back of the boat, because he remembered reading somewhere that oil slicks were a great way of catching sea-creatures. But all they ended up with were a few rather sad-looking seagulls. The pirates felt a little guilty and scooped them up in big nets to give them a clean. The oil didn't come off very well even with lots of scrubbing, so the pirate in red suggested that the oily seagulls might make quite good candles instead. Everybody agreed that this was a good idea, because they had run out of lamp oil.

There was an almighty 'pop' and the pirate with a cauliflower ear disintegrated in an explosion of fireworks. The other pirates 'oohed' and 'aahed' as roman candles and rockets zoomed off into the sky. The pirate with a scarf crossed another item off his clipboard.

'How many schemes is that?' asked the Pirate Captain.

'Fifteen schemes,' said the pirate with a scarf. 'Sixteen if you include the business with the pig.'

'Aaarrr. Best forget that one.'

'It's not going too well, is it, Pirate Captain?' said the scarf-wearing pirate, staring at the conspicuously whaleless sea. 'I'm worried that perhaps this whaling business is a little more difficult than we thought. Possibly that's why Ahab said he'd been chasing the whale for years.'

'Pish,' said the Pirate Captain, trying to sound upbeat. 'What you have to remember is that Ahab never had my maverick sideways approach to problem-solving. It's all in hand.'

He waved that morning's post at the scarf-wearing pirate and started to flick through it.

'Bill, bill, bill, cutlass catalogue, bill . . . Ah-ha! Here we go.' He held up one of the letters triumphantly. 'This'll sort us out, Number Two! I took the precaution of writing to our old friend Scurvy Jake. You know what an outdoors type he is. He even took a job in Brighton Sea Life Centre for a bit whilst he was working his way through pirate academy. So he's bound to know a thing or two about catching fishes! Let's see now . . . "Dear Pirate Captain",' read the Pirate Captain. ' "Thanks for the letter. It's great to hear from you after our last adventure with the monkey wrestling. Since then I've been . . . blah . . . new job as a grill chef . . . blah blah . . . remember the old days . . . blah blah blah . . . might get a new hat . . . blah blah blah blah . . . the most beautiful sunset you can imagine"—good grief, man! Get to the point! Ah, here we are: "About the whale. Interesting question . . . Have you tried dangling that albino chap over the side? Failing that, try magnets! Lots of love, Scurvy Jake".'

The Pirate Captain sighed, and muttered a terrible nautical oath under his breath. He noticed that another of the envelopes had a Nantucket postmark and felt a sudden nasty queasiness deep in his belly. He considered hiding the letter under the astrolabe in his office without reading it, because that was the Pirate Captain's usual way of dealing with letters that he thought might contain bad news, but against his better judgement he opened it up. His salty face turned ashen.

'Is everything okay, Pirate Captain?' asked the scarf-wearing pirate anxiously.

'Aaarrr. Nothing to worry about. It's just a friendly reminder from Cutlass Liz,' said the Pirate Captain, attempting to shoot him a reassuring smile, but finding his mouth stuck in a sort of lop-sided grimace. 'Look here, she's even included a helpful illustration.'

The scarf-wearing pirate looked at the picture on the letterhead, which showed Cutlass Liz merrily dismembering a pirate. There was a speech bubble coming from the pirate's mouth. It said:

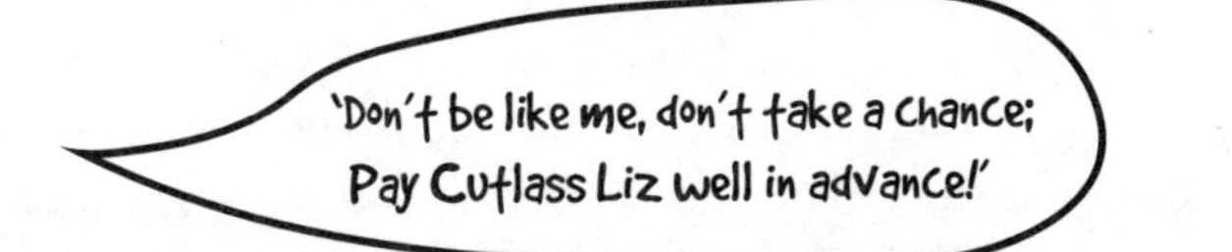

'Don't be like me, don't take a chance;
Pay Cutlass Liz well in advance!'

The Pirate Captain took a few deep breaths and tried to concentrate on calm things, like lapping waves and panpipes. But the vein in his temple was starting to throb, and he could feel a steady panic rising from the soles of his pirate boots.

'I seem to be getting one of my heads,' said the Pirate Captain. And with that he walked very slowly below decks, pausing only briefly to screw Scurvy Jake's letter into a ball and throw it at a passing seagull.

Ten

SWIMMING POOLS OF PASSION!

The pirates lay miserably in their bunks. It had been the best part of a fortnight since they had decided to take up whaling, and they still hadn't seen so much as a blowhole. For the first few days the Pirate Captain had simply glowered and stomped about a bit more than he usually did. But just recently he had started to behave in a more and more alarming fashion. He would spend the nights stalking the deck, muttering darkly to himself, and the days refusing to come out of his cabin. He had taken to bellowing bleak self-penned poetry through the *Lovely Emma*'s speaking tubes. And he hadn't so much as brushed his beard in days. Right at that moment he was stood on the bow of the boat roaring and shaking his fist at the drizzling sky. Normally when the Pirate Captain was in a mood he would have been secretly pleased that the weather reflected it, because the Pirate Captain's moods tended to just be for show. But this was an actual genuine mood, and he wasn't pleased at all.

'Oh dear. He's started shouting at the ocean again,' said the sassy pirate, listening to the faint bellowing sounds that filtered through the porthole.

'I think I prefer the shouting to all that relentless pacing about,' said the pirate in green.

'Or the poetry,' said the pirate with a peg-leg.

'Or the frowning,' said Jennifer.

'Did you see him this morning? I've never seen the vein in his temple get that big before.'

'He told me off for singing a shanty!'

'I took him some beef for dinner. But he wouldn't even let me in. It was specially larded and everything,' said the pirate with a scarf.[27]

'Larded?' said the sassy pirate, licking his lips.

'Yes, glistening with specks of visible fat. I tried wafting the smell under his door, but it was hopeless.'

'I thought I could cheer him up by riding up and down in the dumbwaiter, but he just sat there with his arms folded.'

'No grog. No laughing. Lights out at seven p.m. This isn't what being a pirate is meant to be about at all!'

'We might as well be working in an *office*.'

'I hate whales!'

The pirates all jumped up as their bedroom door was thrown open with a crash.

'Up on deck, you swabs!' roared the Pirate Captain. A couple of the pirates had to fight back tears, because for once it really sounded like the Pirate Captain actually thought they were swabs, and wasn't just saying it to add some colourful nautical atmosphere. The crew all shuffled up the *Lovely Emma*'s spiral staircase and out on to the moonlit deck. The Pirate Captain hadn't even given the pirates time to put on their overcoats and so they had to strain to hear him over their chattering teeth. He pulled a big ham out from under his pirate coat. Not just any old ham, but the Captain's Prize Ham itself. The pirate crew gasped.

---

27 Larded beef (or any meat) has been artificially marbled with fat. Strips of suet or pork fat are run through the lean meat with a 'larding needle' to add extra moisture and flavour.

'Silence!' shouted the Pirate Captain, even though the pirates weren't saying anything. 'Do you see this ham?'

The pirates nodded.

'This is my prize honey-roast ham. Do you see?' he repeated. The pirates nodded again. The Pirate Captain rubbed it with his sleeve to bring up the shine on the glaze and advanced towards the mast with the ham held high.

'Whoever captures the whale, he shall have this ham!'

The Pirate Captain proceeded to nail the ham to the mast. Then he pulled an especially dour face and stormed back downstairs. The pirate crew were left on their own. They looked at each other in dismay.

'His Prize Ham!' said the albino pirate, wide-eyed.

'This is bad,' said the scarf-wearing pirate.

'I don't think I've ever even seen it out of its case before!' said the pirate with gout.

A mixture of emotions ran through the crew. One of the emotions was 'worry', because they realised that things must be pretty serious for the Pirate Captain to take such a drastic step as nailing his ham to the mast. And the other emotion was 'being really hungry', because with its delicious glaze gleaming in the moonlight, the ham looked like just about the loveliest thing any of them had ever seen. So they fetched some blankets to keep warm and sat in a big circle around the mast. Jennifer handed out notepaper to all the pirates so that they could write down their best whale-catching schemes. Some of the pirates rubbed their foreheads really hard to get their brains going, but all it did was make them feel dizzy.

The sun had come up and the pirates were still all sat around in a circle staring at their blank pieces of paper. They had drunk the *Lovely Emma*'s entire supply of coffee, but even that hadn't helped.

'How about something involving semaphore?' said the sassy pirate.

'Does anybody actually know semaphore?' said Jennifer.

Everybody went quiet again.

'It's no good,' said the scarf-wearing pirate, sticking out his lower lip and doodling a little picture of a sad manta ray. 'If the Captain can't come up with a way of catching the whale, then what chance have we got? None of us is as clever as the Captain.'

Even the pirate in red, who normally would have come out with some pithy and sarcastic comment, just nodded in agreement.

'What we need is help,' said Jennifer, 'from somebody just as smart as the Pirate Captain.'

The pirates looked at her dubiously.

'Somebody who's always got a plan. Somebody who is both cunning and ingenious.'

'No!' said the pirate with a scarf, suddenly catching her drift.

'Somebody with a beard that goes all the way up to his eyeballs,' said Jennifer.

'She can't mean!'

'She does!'

'The Pirate Captain will go mad!'

'He's already gone mad,' pointed out Jennifer. 'That's the whole problem.'

The pirates still looked unconvinced.

'I know it's a bit of a risk,' said Jennifer, 'but I for one can't spend another night listening to any more poems with titles like "The Screaming Face of Desolation".'

Eleven

BLOOD, BEER, AND A BUSTED BOAT!

The *Barbary Hen* lay anchored in a beautiful tropical bay that looked like something from a postcard or an expensive jigsaw puzzle. As the *Lovely Emma* pulled up alongside, the pirates could see some of Black Bellamy's crew playing on the beach and splashing about in the sea. The infamous captain seemed to have been recruiting, because there were a number of women in bikinis who the pirates didn't recognise from their previous encounters.

Black Bellamy himself was reclining in a hammock on the deck, drinking grog out of a coconut and talking to a blonde and a brunette. He must have been telling some pretty funny jokes, because the women were laughing at almost everything he said. Seeing the *Lovely Emma*, he waved languidly.

'Hello pirates!' he roared.

'Hello Black Bellamy!' shouted Jennifer. 'Could we have a word?'

'Dear lady! Of course, come aboard,' Black Bellamy shouted back. 'I may be the most diabolical pirate on the Seven Seas, but there's always a welcome on the *Barbary Hen* for a beautiful woman.'

The blonde and the brunette jumped up and placed a gangplank between the two boats, and then wandered off in a leggy way. Black

Bellamy bounded from his hammock and helped Jennifer across. '*Enchanté*,' he said in French, kissing her hand.

'I hope we're not disturbing anything?' said Jennifer.

'Not at all, not at all. We're just taking a bit of shore leave after the Vegas run. Maxing and relaxing, that kind of thing,' said Black Bellamy, looking across at the *Lovely Emma*. 'It really is a nice boat you've got there, you know. Puts the *Barbary Hen* to shame. Tell me—was it the Pirate Captain's idea to put all those bits of squid in the rigging? And wrap that dead eel around the bow?'

'Um, sort of. Actually, Mister Bellamy, it's the Pirate Captain I need to talk to you about,' said Jennifer. 'He's gone a bit loopy.'

'Oh good grief! My poor old friend!' said Black Bellamy, putting his hand to his brow in horror. 'Well, we must discuss this properly. Over dinner. Come into my office and we'll talk all about it.'

Black Bellamy took Jennifer's hand and led her downstairs to his office. He opened the door with a flourish and waved her in. Nobody had held a door open for Jennifer since she'd left Victorian London.[28] She was very impressed. Black Bellamy had somehow managed to combine lavish ostentation with aesthetic restraint. The furniture was pretty classy stuff like chaise-longues and glass coffee tables, and Jennifer noticed several oil paintings that were of an even better quality than the ones in the Pirate Captain's office. There was Black Bellamy with his arm round the Emperor Ninko of Japan. And there he was with the eighteen-year-old Isabella II of Spain, holding up fish and fishing rods by a river—this one was signed 'With love to my main pirate, Izzi XXX'. There was a well-stocked trophy cabinet against one wall, with a couple of 'Beard Wearer of the Year' awards, and on the opposite wall he had a display case marked 'Rare Bird Eggs', full of dozens and dozens of peregrine falcon eggs. The whole room was suffused by the faint smell of seaweed.

---

28 Gentlemen opening doors for Victorian ladies was not just a matter of manners. The big skirts and dresses of the day meant that a lady would be unable to get in and out of carriages and rooms unless someone held the door open in advance.

Jennifer spotted a photograph of Black Bellamy's class from pirate academy sitting on his desk. She was surprised to see that even as a young pirate his beard went right up to his eyeballs. More surprising still was who was stood next to him. It was the Pirate Captain. His belly was perhaps a little less impressive, and he didn't have quite so many gold teeth, but it was definitely him.

'I didn't realise you'd known the Pirate Captain so long!' exclaimed Jennifer.

'Oh yes, we go way back,' said Black Bellamy, handing her a glass of rum. 'I think you'll find this a passable vintage. I'm told 1812 was a good year for grog.'

'So you were at school together?' asked Jennifer, her curiosity piqued.

'We were even roommates for a while. We were like *that*!' said Black Bellamy, crossing his fingers.

'But the Pirate Captain's always saying that you're his archnemesis and you don't miss an opportunity to mess him about, and that you're diabolical beyond measure,' said Jennifer.

'It's just banter, Jennifer. He's an old rogue!' replied Black Bellamy with a laugh.

Two of Black Bellamy's pirates brought in a selection of oysters and some other fancy shellfish.

'But enough about me,' said Black Bellamy, 'let's talk about you. How can I help *you*?'

'It's not me, Mister Bellamy . . . it's the Captain. He's got himself all wound up about catching this whale. He's not himself.'

'Poor Pirate Captain. You've got really nice earrings, by the way. Nice and sparkly.'

'Thanks, that's very kind. So have you. But—uh—like I was saying. The Pirate Captain. He's not even *eating* properly.'

'Yes, yes. Sorry to hear that—you're quite a distraction, you know,' said Black Bellamy.

'The thing is, we've tried to catch the whale to cheer him up, but we don't really know where to start. They're slippery creatures, these whales.'

'I can imagine. Now, you're a Gemini, aren't you?'

'Oh no, I'm a Leo.'

'I knew it! I can always tell. Your fiery lips give you away.'

'Really? You do say some things, Mister Bellamy.'

Black Bellamy leaned back in his chair, which served to show off his expansively hairy chest. He dabbed at his temple with a napkin. 'Is it just me, or is it rather hot in here?' he said.

'It is quite warm, yes.'

'Feel free to take a few of those layers off if you're uncomfortable.'

As the meal wore on, Jennifer began to think that Black Bellamy wasn't quite the villain she had been led to believe. He was certainly courteous, always leaning forward eagerly when she tried to reach a dish, or complimenting her on the way she held a fork. He was a good listener too, ever-ready with a compliment and extremely interested in her life and dress sizes. Admittedly, he was surprisingly clumsy—she lost count of the number of times he accidentally knocked the pepperpot to the floor and she had to bend over to pick it up. But really he wasn't such a bad sort at all.

'. . . and that's how I nursed that little kitten back to health,' said Black Bellamy at the end of a story. He cradled his hairy chin in his hand and looked thoughtfully into Jennifer's eyes.

'How wonderful,' said Jennifer, clapping. 'That's very similar to a story that the Pirate Captain tells about a kitten. Oh! The Pirate Captain! I'd almost forgotten why I was here!'

Black Bellamy muttered something under his breath.

'So can you help? Can you?'

Black Bellamy puffed out his cheeks. 'I'm very flattered you should ask. But what makes you think that I might succeed where such a clever young woman has failed? I'm just an unassuming pirate trying to make his way in the world like everybody else.'

'Oh no! Everybody knows how clever you are!'

'Oh *don't*! Really? What do they say?'

'The men are always saying how you're "confounded clever" and how your "cunning is surpassed only by the devil himself". Someone called you an evil genius!'

'I really can't believe that,' said Black Bellamy. Jennifer thought he was probably blushing underneath all that beard. 'Besides, I'd like to think I'm more of a "jovial nuisance" than an "evil genius". But this whale business—I'll see what I can do. When a lovely lady like yourself comes to ask, I can hardly refuse, can I?'

'Oh wow! Thanks Black Bellamy!' Jennifer leapt up and kissed him on the forehead. Then she held up her glass of grog. 'Let's drink to friendship!'

'Friendship! And ladies' faces!' roared Black Bellamy.

When Jennifer and Black Bellamy reappeared on the deck of the *Barbary Hen* they both waved at the pirates anxiously waiting on the *Lovely Emma*.

'He's going to help!' she said, hugging Black Bellamy. She ignored the immature pirates who went 'woooooo!' when they saw the hug.

'Thanks, Black Bellamy!' said the scarf-wearing pirate, helping Jennifer back across the plank. 'We won't forget this in a hurry!'

'It's nothing,' shouted Black Bellamy, as the *Barbary Hen* began to sail off. 'It's just so awful to hear that the Pirate Captain has gone a bit mental. When I think of his poor little mad face, I feel quite emotional.'

The pirates barely had time to get even halfway through an exciting game of Scrabble before the *Barbary Hen* sailed back into view. They all crowded around the boat's telescope and fought to see what was going on.

'He's back already!' said the albino pirate.

'He can't be!' said the pirate in red.

'He is! I don't believe it! And he's got the whale!' exclaimed the pirate with a scarf.

As the *Barbary Hen* came closer they could see Black Bellamy leaning nonchalantly on the ship's wheel, steering with one hand and examining the nails of his other. And there behind him, sat right in the middle of the deck, was a gigantic white whale strapped down by hefty nautical ropes. The whale flapped its tail and a steaming jet of spray erupted from its blowhole, catching the sunlight in a rainbow haze. It was an impressive-looking creature, thought the pirate with a scarf. He remembered how Charles Darwin, the young naturalist they had encountered on their previous adventure, had told him that if you got yourself twelve sets of pirate lungs and then stitched them all together, disgusting though it would be, they would still have just half the lung capacity of one of a whale's lungs. That wasn't the kind of statistic to be taken lightly.

'That Black Bellamy,' said the pirate with a hook for a hand. 'You've got to hand it to him, he's pretty good at stuff.'

Jennifer clapped her hands. 'Somebody go and get the Captain! He'll be over the moon!'

The pirate with a scarf ran down the stairs and came back a few moments later, followed by what the crew at first glance thought must be a dirty old tramp. The pirates all gasped when they realised that the shuffling, shabby mess wasn't a tramp—it was the Pirate Captain, wearing only a pair of grubby pyjama bottoms. His eyes were wild and staring, his face was anything but pleasant or open, and his beard was ratty and unmanageable. Blinking at the light, the Pirate Captain stared uncomprehendingly about. But as the *Barbary Hen* pulled up alongside the *Lovely Emma*, he spotted the whale and his mouth fell open.

'The white whale!' he croaked. Then he saw Black Bellamy. 'And you, you scoundrel!'

'Pirate Captain!' said Jennifer crossly. 'I'm so sorry, Mister Bellamy. He doesn't know what he's saying.' She turned back to the Pirate Captain. 'You're being very rude to Mister Bellamy.'

'No, no,' said Black Bellamy. 'It's quite understandable.' He looked sadly at his shoes. 'I know we've had our ups and downs, Pirate Captain. And I know that I've not been entirely honest with you in the past. But I'd just like you to think of this as a favour from an old friend. Your men told me that you were having a tough time of it and this seemed the least I could do.'

The Pirate Captain was really very touched. It was all he could do to try to stop his voice sounding too emotional. 'I don't know what to say,' he said.

'Then don't say anything at all, Pirate Captain,' said Black Bellamy, putting a finger to his lips. 'Except,' he added, 'there is just one small matter.' Black Bellamy paused. 'Obviously I went to the trouble of finding the whale for no more reward than to see my dear friend get back to his old self. But on my way here I happened to receive a heart-rending letter from some orphans. They need me to go and stop their orphanage being knocked down by greedy real-estate developers.'

'That's awful!' said the albino pirate.

'I know. I think of those orphans and I well up. I do,' said Black Bellamy, dabbing at the beard below his eyes. 'So, although I'd love to let you have the whale for nothing, I'd be grateful if you could just pay a nominal sum that I can then pass on to the orphans. To help them in their hour of need. I wouldn't even ask otherwise.'

'We haven't got much,' said the pirate with a scarf. 'Just the money we made from our Vegas show.'

Black Bellamy shrugged. 'Well, I'm sure those cripples will be very grateful for anything.'

'Cripples? I thought you said that they were orphans?' said Jennifer.

'Ah,' said Black Bellamy, 'orphan cripples, my dear. Terrible business. And some of them have the pox. Orphan cripple pox victims.'

The Pirate Captain felt so moved by Black Bellamy's devotion to the needy that he threw in the big stone coin and their few remaining limes as well. Black Bellamy grinned, pocketed the loot, and hopped back across to his boat.

'Make sure you feed him three times a day or he gets a bit restless,' he said as the crew of the *Barbary Hen* finished heaving the white whale onto the deck of the *Lovely Emma*. 'And above all else, whatever you do, *don't get him wet*. Whales hate getting wet, Pirate Captain.'

'But what about all that time they spend cavorting around in the ocean?' said the Pirate Captain. 'They love getting wet.'

'You'd think so, wouldn't you?' said Black Bellamy, laughing. 'But it's an old myth. They're mammals, remember? Just the same as you or me. Or a cow. And how many times have you seen a cow go for a swim?'

'I suppose you're right,' said the Pirate Captain. 'I'd never thought of it like that.'

And so the two sets of pirates said their goodbyes and set sail in different directions, Black Bellamy to help the orphan cripples and the Pirate Captain to Nantucket to collect Ahab's reward.

'That's a stroke of luck, eh lads?' said the Pirate Captain, turning to the crew.

'Are you feeling better now, Captain?' asked the albino pirate.

'One of the advantages of having a temperament as unpredictable as mine is that you get over things like stress and depression extremely quickly.'

'Captain Ahab will be really pleased,' said the pirate with gout, giving the whale a pat.

'The only thing is, it's not as big as I was expecting, Captain,' said the pirate in red, looking at the creature waggle its little flippers. 'I mean, Ahab made quite an issue about it being a leviathan. But it's really more a sort of middling-sized whale.'

'Aaarrr. He struck me as the type to exaggerate,' said the Pirate Captain breezily. 'Didn't he tell us that he'd combed every *inch* of the sea? That's obviously impossible—especially since Black Bellamy found him after twenty minutes! And besides, how many white whales could there possibly be knocking about?'

The pirates nodded.

'Now, I know I smell a bit ripe, so I'm off for a nice long soaky bath. You might want to air my duvets, Number Two.'

Twelve

I FOUGHT THE SARGASSO SQUID!

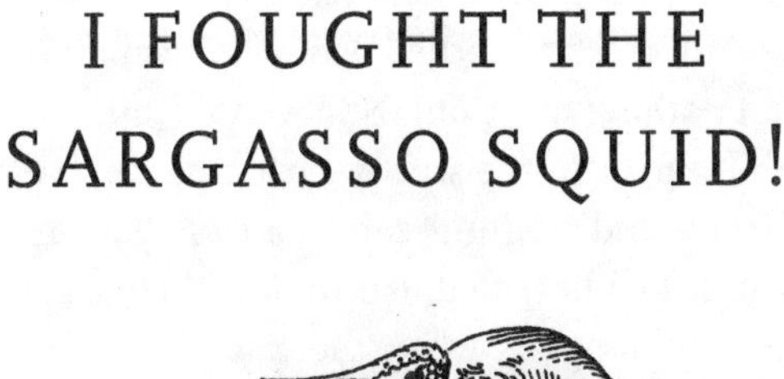

'Take that, pirate boat! Now I, the terrible sponge, am master of this ocean!'

The Pirate Captain was sat in the bath, and as always he was putting on a bit of a show whilst the scarf-wearing pirate scrubbed him clean. He made a sort of glugging noise and sank the sextant that was doubling as a pirate boat once and for all.

'It's a good job there aren't really gigantic sponge creatures about, isn't it?' he said, waggling the victorious sponge at his deputy. 'Or us pirates would be done for.'[29]

'You're right, sir. I often think just that.'

'But it's a shame the sea can't be full of lovely bubbles like this.'

'It *is* a shame,' agreed the pirate with a scarf sadly. His rugged brow was furrowed in concentration as he carefully soaped each delicate strand of the Pirate Captain's beard. He stood up and surveyed his handiwork.

'I think we can rinse her off now, Captain.'

---

29 Sponges are amongst the simplest multicellular animals—loose collections of specialised cells combined to produce a more efficient feeding mechanism. They range from inconspicuous prickly layers growing on rocks to large, complex and beautiful structures such as Venus's flower-basket. None are capable of attacking a ship.

'I hope she's going to be okay,' grimaced the Pirate Captain, gently supporting his soapy beard in his hands. 'Can't remember a time when I've let her get into such a mess.'

The pirate with a scarf reached across to turn on one of the big brass taps, but nothing came out. Not even a drop.

'That's not right,' said the scarf-wearing pirate. He tried to turn on the other tap, and nothing came out of that one either. The Pirate Captain looked horrified. He couldn't help but think back to their adventure in Tangiers when the water in the hotel at which the pirates were staying had given out and the Captain had been left in the same situation, completely unable to rinse out his beard except with seawater. Over the next couple of days it had puffed up into a ridiculous frizzy ball, and he had ended up looking more like one of those hats that Russian spy ladies wear than a respected old sea-dog.

So the Pirate Captain leapt from his tub and bounded onto the deck to try and find out what was amiss, naked as a newborn baby, except a good deal hairier and with a few more tattoos. For those readers who may be interested, the Pirate Captain's tattoos included:

- A map of an island across his belly. This had a big 'X' on it, which the Captain thought probably had something to do with treasure. Unfortunately, he had no idea where the island was, because like most of his tattoos, it was the product of an evening full of too much grog. He had just woken up in Portsmouth one morning and there it was.

- The Pirate King's face on his right bicep. He'd grown since it was done and now the tattoo was a bit misshapen, so that the Pirate King looked a little bit like he'd had a stroke.

- A picture of an anchor on his left forearm. This was to remind the Pirate Captain to drop anchor whenever they were leaving the boat. Otherwise it just tended to drift off, and the men would look at him accusingly.

- A shopping list on his shin, which had seemed like a good idea at the time.
- 'I've seen the lions at Longleat' on his left shoulder blade.
- 'Left' on his left foot and 'Right' on his right. A gift from his mother on his fourth birthday.

There the Pirate Captain stood, like a perfectly proportioned nude renaissance statue. He had always been extremely comfortable with his own naked body, but some of the pirate crew seemed quite overwhelmed by the sheer soapy spectacle. Looking about, hands on hips, it was instantly obvious to the Captain what the problem was. Somehow the wily whale had managed to slip from its moorings, and was now flopping about on the deck, causing all sorts of mischief. There were bits of broken barrel and squashed pirate everywhere. Most of the flower beds in the ornamental garden were ruined, and there was a big plume of water coming from where the whale had managed to bash a jagged hole in one of the *Lovely Emma*'s water pipes with a particularly vicious flick of its tail. The water that was meant for the Pirate Captain's beard was fountaining onto the deck, and raining down on the whale. The Captain watched in dismay as the creature began to change from a pearly white to a battleship grey. A great big puddle of paint collected around the base of the whale and seeped towards the Pirate Captain's toes.

'Don't get it wet,' he muttered to himself. 'That Black Bellamy. He's . . . he's . . .'

'The living end?' suggested the pirate in red.

'Exactly.' The Pirate Captain made a mental note to get a new tattoo that said something terrible about Black Bellamy's mother.

'He didn't find the white whale at all! We've been duped! The cove probably just stole this regular whale from the nearest zoo!'

The Pirate Captain paced around the creature. 'Well, lads,' he said. 'We'll just have to slap on some more paint and hope that Ahab doesn't look at the thing too closely. You and you,' he pointed at the pirate in red and the new pirate with an accordion, 'Come on, you cozening brace of dandies! You're on whale-painting detail.'

None of the pirates was particularly good at plumbing, so the Captain had to finish washing his beard off in the spray of water bursting from the broken pipe. Then he went downstairs and, after getting dressed, spending a few minutes tying ribbons in his beard and practising some victorious faces for the benefit of Cutlass Liz, the Pirate Captain strode back onto the deck to see how the whale painting was going. He was glad to see that they'd managed to paint about half of the beast's great face a nice shade of 'Orchid Haze'. The effect was only spoilt by the elegantly curled moustache and big bushy eyebrows that the whale was now sporting. The Pirate Captain had a pretty good idea as to whose handiwork this was.

'You!' he said, pointing at the pirate in red. 'What are you playing at?'

The pirate in red sidled guiltily along a flipper.

'I just thought it gave him a bit of character,' he said. 'I was going to paint a little top hat as well. To make him a gentleman whale.'

'I'll paint you a new *@#*&!' roared the Pirate Captain. It wasn't often that he used language, but the pirate in red had been riding his luck for the whole adventure.

'You're always saying we should express ourselves creatively,' whined the pirate in red.

'Scrub it off! Right now, you cove!'

The Pirate Captain folded his arms and contemplated the whale. He looked across at his trusty deputy.

'What do you think, Number Two?' said the Pirate Captain. 'Not quite there, is it?'

'Hard to say, Captain,' said the pirate with a scarf.

'I mean—Ahab may be a monomaniacal old bore, but he doesn't

look like he'd be easily cheated.' The Pirate Captain's eyebrows drooped a bit.

'No, sir. He's a bit of a stickler for detail, I'd say.'

The two pirates fell into a thoughtful silence and stared at the shiny white whale. Then a wily look crept over the Pirate Captain's face.

'You know what would help, Number Two?'

'What's that, Captain?'

'If this whale were to *confess* to being the whale who ate Ahab's leg.'

The pirate with a scarf pulled a bit of a face, and not for the first time wondered if his Captain might not have been spending a bit too much time under tropical suns of late.

'No, hear me out,' said the Pirate Captain, catching his look. 'Do you remember the story of Jonah?'

'Not really, sir.'

'Well, the gist of the thing is that back in biblical times a man goes to live inside a whale for a bit. I forget the exact reason, probably to avoid having to make boat repayments. Not much of a story, but that's the Bible for you.'

'Are you going anywhere with this, Captain?'

'All it needs is for one of us pirates to hide inside the belly of the whale. That way if old Ahab raises any doubts about the veracity of our catch, the swallowed pirate can loudly proclaim how he's the very same whale that ate his leg off. To the outside world it will seem that it's the whale doing the talking, especially if we devise some kind of apparatus to move the whale's mouth up and down while the pirate speaks. Lip-synching the thing will be the key. If you can call it lip-synching, seeing as I don't think whales can be described as having any lips to speak of.'

There was a bit of an argument between the pirates as to whether whales had lips *per se*, with the conclusion being that whilst they had definite edges to their mouths, they were more like gums than lips. A couple of the pirates started work on building the lip/gum-synching apparatus, whilst the Captain lined up the rest of the crew beside the creature.

'Right, me beauties. I'll be needing a volunteer to slither down the whale's fishy throat. You know me—normally I'd be first to step forward, but it'll look pretty suspicious if I'm not there to hand him over, won't it? So—who's it going to be?'

The pirates did their usual trick of staring at the horizon and pretending not to hear.

'Sometimes I think I'd be better off crewing the ship with lobsters,' said the Pirate Captain, with a sorry shake of his head. 'Well then. We'll decide this like pirates. You in the green . . . you can start.' He nodded at the pirate in green.

'I went to the shops and I bought a cutlass,' said the pirate in green.

'I went to the shops,' said the sassy pirate, 'and I bought a cutlass and some brass buckles.'

'I went to the shops,' said the albino pirate, 'and I bought a cutlass, some brass buckles, and some transfers . . .'

It wasn't the fastest way to reach a decision and in the past it had proved costly in battle situations, but the Pirate Captain was a stickler for pirate traditions. Technically it was the pirate with a squint who made the first mistake, but the Pirate Captain decided to send the pirate in red inside the whale, because he was sick of his surly backchat.

'Can I take a magazine to read?' said the pirate in red, clambering into the whale's gaping maw.

'Sorry, lad. No light in there, is there? You'll ruin your eyes,' said the Pirate Captain cheerily. 'Mind your head on the epiglottis!' he added, giving the pirate in red an encouraging shove.

An eerie keening sound washed across the deck as the pirate in red headed for the gloom of the whale's innards.

'What in the blue blazes is that racket?' said the Pirate Captain.

'I think it's whale song!' said Jennifer.

'It's beautiful!' said the pirate in green, entranced.

'We can't just give him to Ahab to chop up! Not a noble creature like this, capable of such magnificent music!' said the pirate with a poetic bent.

'It's just *moaning*,' said the Pirate Captain, snorting and pulling an unimpressed face.

'Couldn't we get him to apologise to Ahab as well?' said Jennifer. 'He could say, "Sorry about the leg, Ahab. Accidents happen. No hard feelings, eh?" and then Ahab might let him off.'

The Pirate Captain rolled his eyes, because if there was one thing guaranteed to make his crew go gooey, it was creatures. The pirates had once spent an entire adventure pestering the Captain to buy them a parrot, only for him to find it two weeks later being used as a fuse on one of the boat's cannons. But by this point in his piratical career he had learnt that there wasn't much point arguing with the lads once they had their hearts set on something.

'*Fine*. If it really makes you feel better,' said the Pirate Captain, rubbing his temples wearily. 'Just so long as we convince Ahab he's the real deal. He can do the Gettysburg Address for all I care.'

Thirteen

CANNIBAL CORAL CRAWLS TO KILL!

The Nantucket town clock struck a quarter to midnight as the last few bits of ground-up pirate bone ran through Cutlass Liz's egg-timer.

'Put your backs into it, boys!' said the Pirate Captain. 'You're doing a great job. Obviously I'd love to help you drag the whale onto the docks, but its oily hide could do lasting damage to my magnificent beard. And us pirates without my beard would be like the Tower of London without those big crows—we'd most likely just collapse in a heap.'

The crew let out a collective grunt and with a final heave pushed the whale over the side of the *Lovely Emma* and onto the dock's slippery cobblestones. Mindful that good pirating is all about the spectacle, the Pirate Captain had covered the creature with a big white sheet, so that he could unveil their prize with a flourish.

There was quite a crowd waiting for them. Ahab and his whalers were there, stony-faced as ever. Cutlass Liz was there, tapping her watch and looking cross. And there were a few assorted hangers-on who had just turned up to see what all the fuss was about.

'I hope you've got me here for a good reason,' said Ahab, looking moody in pyjamas and nightcap.

'Where's my money?' said Cutlass Liz, pointedly sharpening a big knife on a leather strap. 'And what have you got under that sheet?'

'The answer to all our problems!' said the Pirate Captain triumphantly, and with a theatrical jerk of his wrist he pulled the billowing sheet aside. There was a bit of a stunned silence.

'That's not six thousand doubloons,' said Cutlass Liz.

'It's a whale!' said the albino pirate helpfully.

'And not just any whale!' said the Pirate Captain, pointing at Ahab. 'But the brute who ate your leg off!'

Ahab looked the creature up and down. He circled round it a couple of times. He got out a little pair of half-moon spectacles and peered at it closely.

'I'm not convinced,' he muttered.

The Pirate Captain shrugged. 'I thought you might say that, but I can prove it.' He gave the sassy pirate a wink to get him ready with the lip-synching device. 'Because this whale will confess to the crime himself!'

'Pardon?' said Ahab.

'Isn't that so, whale? You've got something to say? Hmmm?' said the Pirate Captain, playing to the crowd a little as the sassy pirate started to work the ingenious system of pulleys and gears and bits of rope that made the whale's jaw jerk up and down.

'I have, Pirate Captain!' said the whale in what to the onlookers seemed a surprisingly reedy voice for such a huge beast.

'He's not as good at doing voices as me,' the Pirate Captain whispered to the scarf-wearing pirate. 'Though to be fair, it's difficult to sound genuinely oceanic.'

'First,' said the whale/pirate, 'I'd like to say how underrated the pirate in red is. In my whale's opinion I would say he is the best pirate in the whole crew.'

The Pirate Captain scowled, because this wasn't exactly the way they'd rehearsed it.

'One of the reasons he's so good is that he bothers to learn the proper nautical terms for things, and can tell the difference between the galley and the steering wheel. Can you do that, Pirate Captain?'

'Aarrrr,' said the Pirate Captain defensively. 'Of course.'

'I mean to say, you wouldn't have any problem telling the mizzen-mast from the foremast? And you'd never be heard referring to the hull as "that bit which stops all the water getting in"?'

The Pirate Captain started to finger his cutlass in what he hoped was a menacing fashion, but then he remembered that just because the pirate was inside the whale it didn't mean he could *see* what the whale could see, so using a subtle visual threat was probably useless.

'And another reason the pirate in red is so good is because he has an imperious nose. Not, you notice, a "stentorian" nose because stentorian is a tone of voice.'

'Well, whale, I'm sure we all agree with you about how fantastic the pirate in red is,' said the Pirate Captain, through gritted gold teeth. 'It would certainly be a shame if anything terrible happened to him. Like, oh I don't know, spending the rest of our next adventure getting keel-hauled.[30] Or fed to sea cucumbers. Now, I think you have a message for Mister Ahab, don't you?'

'All right, I was getting to it,' said the whale/pirate testily. 'Ahab—I just wanted to say how sorry I am about the business when I ate your leg. I'd got a bit bored that day of plankton or squid or whatever it is I usually eat. I hope there's no hard feelings.'

The sassy pirate surreptitiously used the lip-synching apparatus to make the whale do a winning and apologetic grin. There was an expectant hush.

'Well,' said Ahab, scratching his scar, 'I suppose this must be the beast. Though he seems to have shrunk since I saw him last.'

'That's seawater for you,' said the Pirate Captain, thinking fast. 'I once dropped my favourite blousy shirt into a rock pool, and by the time I fished the thing out it wouldn't have fitted a baby.'

Ahab still looked slightly unconvinced.

30 Keel-hauling was actually a practice used more by the Royal Navy than pirates, and it was an attempt to escape this kind of barbarity that probably drove many sailors into piracy in the first place.

The Pirate Captain hurriedly looked at his pocket watch. 'So then. It appears that just for once we've finished with a bit of time to spare. All that's left is for you'—he grinned as hopefully as he could at Ahab—'to give us our reward, so that I can pay you'—he grinned as sexily as he could at Cutlass Liz—'and then I can spend the rest of the adventure just messing about with my belly.'

But before the Pirate Captain could even begin to play about with his belly button, the whole dock started to shake, and there was a sound like a thousand cannonballs being dropped into a bucket. A wall of water rose up from the sea and crashed across the docks. Out from the churning swell came the tip of something white, and it kept on coming until there, rearing up on its tail, was the biggest whale any of the pirates had ever seen. If the pirates had been alive a hundred and fifty years later and had happened to be drawing the diagrams in biology textbooks, they would have said the whale was as tall as three double-decker buses stacked on top of each other, or about a half of one St Paul's Cathedral. But they weren't, so they just thought that the whale was really very big indeed.

The monster roared, lunged and came crashing down right on top of the *Lovely Emma*. All the onlookers scattered about, and most of the pirates tried to hide behind barrels.

'Oh dear,' said the Pirate Captain.

'Goodness me,' said the pirate with a scarf.

The whale rose up again, and with another resounding thump belly-flopped onto the boat.

'This is a bit of bad luck, isn't it, Captain?' said the pirate with gout.

'I hate to say I told you so,' said the fake whale/pirate in red, 'but if you will go about the place killing albatrosses, you have to expect this kind of thing.'

Just for once the Pirate Captain found himself agreeing with the mutinous swab. It did seem like a spectacular piece of cosmic bad luck for the white whale to turn up out of the blue like this, apparently for no better reason than to make his life a misery. He stared sadly at the *Lovely Emma*. Then he stared at the whale. A huge excited whale eye winked back at him. The Pirate Captain stared at the *Lovely Emma* again. And suddenly everything clicked into place in his piratical brain.

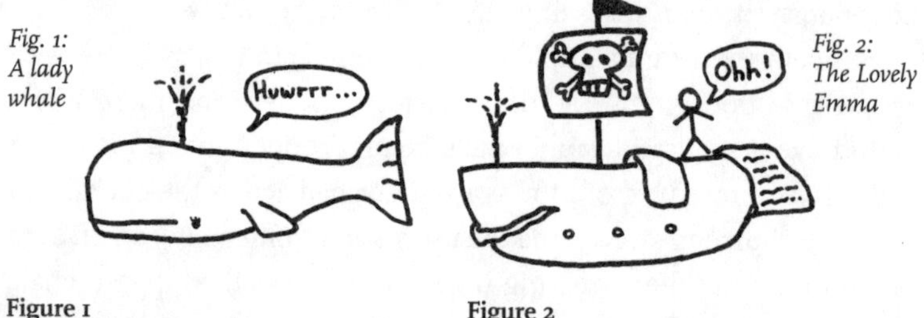

Figure 1
Gigantic tail
Colossal flipper
Flirtatious mouth
Spray from the blowhole
The gentle echo of whale song

Figure 2
The banner from the Las Vegas show
The Captain's duvet put out to air
Dead eel wrapped around the bow
Burst waterpipe
A moaning leper

'The beast thinks our boat is a lady whale!' he cried.

There was a terrible creaking noise, and the *Lovely Emma* lurched this way and that.

'I don't think the boat is enjoying it all that much,' said the pirate with a scarf.

'But why would the man whale want to squash a lady whale like that?' asked the albino pirate. The Pirate Captain didn't think now was the moment to explain, because a horrifying thought suddenly flashed into his magnificent head: the Prize Ham was still nailed to the *Lovely Emma*'s mast.

'My ham! My beautiful ham!' roared the Pirate Captain. And before he had really thought things through, he found himself charging towards the *Lovely Emma* in a panic.

'What on earth is the fellow doing?' said Ahab, as the Captain streaked towards the boat.

'He's decided to show that whale who's boss!' exclaimed Jennifer. 'Yay! Go Pirate Captain!'

'Shouldn't you be doing that too, Mister Ahab?' said the pirate with long legs. 'Because of all of the cold-revenge-soothing-the-soul business?'

Ahab looked at the terrible gaping maw of the whale, and at its appalling chomping teeth. 'For some reason,' he said, 'upon seeing the beast, I do not find myself so inclined.'

'Is your Captain always like this?' asked Cutlass Liz, shaking her head in disbelief.

'Oh yes,' said the pirate in green confidently. 'He's very brave. He once took on the entire Royal Navy single-handed, whilst we were all asleep. They boarded us in the dead of night and stole our last few bottles of grog, and then the Pirate Captain fought them off but he was too late to save the grog. We didn't even know a thing about it until the next morning when we realised the grog was gone and he explained what had happened to us over breakfast. The whole fight had given him a terrible headache.'

About fifteen feet from the jetty, the Pirate Captain began to appreciate just how massive the white whale was. He himself was rightly famed across the Seven Seas for being able to fit an entire pork chop in his mouth, but the beast in whose shadow all the pirates now cowered looked as if it could fit an entire field of cows in its mouth all in one go, and maybe still have room to spare. Wondering just how wise it would be to interrupt something so gigantic right in the middle of it getting busy[31]—even for a cause as noble as saving his ham—the Pirate Captain reconsidered and did his best to try skidding to a halt, but the cobblestones were even more slippery now, and instead of stopping, the Captain simply went sliding right off the side of the dock and into the cold sea with a plaintive 'plop'.

[31] Different types of whales adopt different reproductive strategies. Male humpback whales sometimes blow a thick curtain of bubbles to try and block their intended mate from the view of other competing males. Whilst uninterested females have been observed to hide under boats and wait there until the males have all gone away. Smart creatures, male whales have never been observed trying to impress lady whales by writing books about pirates.

'Oh no,' said the pirate with a scarf, looking on distraught. 'I can't bear to look.'

The monstrous whale went on bouncing up and down on the boat. The onlookers gazed apprehensively at the churning sea, but there was no sign of the Captain.

'Arrrr,' muttered Ahab broodingly into the middle distance. 'That was a brave way to go. The good Captain must have known his was a path that could end only with the hangman's noose, or the murky depths of the ocean. Yet he paid it no mind! To risk everything in the pursuit of liberty and pleasure without constraint. Isn't that the very reason why he chose the life of a pirate?'

'Not really,' said the albino pirate, fighting back the tears. 'I think it was more just something to do.'

The water in the harbour was very dark. Not for the first time it occurred to the Pirate Captain that, given his line of work, he really should have learnt to swim by now. At one point he had actually spent entire adventures wearing armbands just in case this kind of situation cropped up, but somehow it never really struck the right bloodthirsty note. He flapped his arms uselessly for a while and then started to sink like a brick. A piece of seaweed got tangled up in his beard, and a little shoal of fish bobbed past his face. He was trying to decide if he would prefer '*A man like no other*' or '*He was a true original*' as the inscription on his gravestone, when he felt himself rush up through the water, break the surface, and fly through the air in a burst of spray. The white whale had waggled its great tail and flipped the Pirate Captain as if he were nothing more than a soggy pinball. He described a perfect piratical arc before coming thumping down onto the deck of the *Lovely Emma*. The Captain sat there for a moment, shook the kelp from his beard and looked about him in a daze.

'He's back!' cheered the pirate in green.

'And he's not even hurrying,' said the pirate with a hook for a hand. 'I'd like to see Black Bellamy stay that nonchalant when his boat was being attacked by the biggest whale in the world.'

As the Pirate Captain's vision cleared, he saw that he had landed right next to the mast where his Prize Ham was still nailed. He staggered to his feet, pulled out the nail, grabbed the ham in both arms and gave it a big hug. 'I'll never leave you alone again,' he promised in a hoarse whisper. The whale chose this touching moment to do a particularly energetic belly flop onto the *Lovely Emma*'s aft, which sent her lurching sharply. The Pirate Captain hooked one arm around the mast and wondered what to do. He considered punching the whale on the nose, because he recalled something about that being their weak spot. But then he remembered how that might be sharks rather than whales. And also that it was probably apocryphal anyway. And of course whales don't really have noses.

The whale went on writhing about, half on the ship and half off. Its great twisted mouth was clashing and biting alarmingly close to the Pirate Captain now, and he swore he caught a glimpse of the remains of Ahab's leg trapped in one of the sharp molars. The creature snapped its jaws shut barely inches from where he was standing, and the Pirate Captain let out a terrified shriek and leapt into the air. He landed with a squelch on the whale's eyelid and clung on for dear life.

'Did you hear that high-pitched roar of defiance as he jumped onto its face?' said Jennifer.

'That,' said Ahab, 'is the most courageous man I ever saw.'

With a loud and slightly obscene groan, the beast started to slide back into the water. The Pirate Captain realised that his only chance now was to try and scale the fish's face and leap across the dock. He scrambled desperately against its rubbery flesh, hauling himself up inch by inch, but just as he was scrabbling for a handhold on the whale's furrowed brow, his shiny pirate boot skated across its skin and let out a horrendous squeak. It was a lot like when someone does that trick of scraping their nails down a blackboard. The Pirate Captain's sensitive teeth were so set on edge by this that he clamped his hands to his ears, and in the process dropped his Prize Ham. It bounced away down the whale's back.

'Hell's bells!' exclaimed the Pirate Captain, sprinting along the top of the whale in pursuit. For one moment he thought he had it, but the ham flipped through the air and, with a sudden *sucking* sound, bounced straight into the whale's blowhole. The Captain knelt down and desperately tried to wiggle it free, but the thing was stuck fast.

'Come on, Pirate Captain!' cheered the watching pirates. 'This is no time for a snack. Give that whale a smack!'

As the Pirate Captain strained at the ham, the whale began to spasm and buck about in the water. Its tail thrashed wildly up and down. Its flippers windmilled in the air uselessly. Then an ear-splitting moan erupted from its mouth and the whale rolled from the sinking boat onto the dock, shuddering one last terrible death spasm before lying still on the cobbles.

The Pirate Captain slid down its cheek and landed in front of the crowd of pirates and onlookers. They all started clapping, so he did a little bow.

'That was brilliant!' said the pirate with a scarf.

'You've killed the white whale!' exclaimed Ahab.

'How did you know what to do, Captain?' said the albino pirate.

'Aaarrrr,' said the Captain, emptying some seawater from his hat. 'Well. As I may have pointed out before, I'm not a *complete* idiot, you know.'

The crowd all looked at him expectantly. The Pirate Captain thought for a bit and then put on an authoritative tone of voice. 'Any seafaring type knows that the blowhole of the whale is essential for expelling whale wee. It was clear to me that if I could block the blow-hole, the whale's bladder would swell up and explode.'

'And the way you made it look like you were really quite hapless whilst you were doing it,' said Cutlass Liz, with a playful slap of his shoulder, 'so that the whale wouldn't cotton on to your clever plan. Genius, Captain.'

'*That* was the beast who ate my leg,' said Ahab, pointing to the dead whale.

'Arrrr. This probably looks bad,' said the Captain apologetically, 'but I can explain.'

Ahab wasn't listening. 'I am afraid, Pirate Captain, that you have been had. This creature,' and he pointed at the pirates' fake whale, 'has been masquerading as the real villain, even though he is innocent of the crime.'

Ahab turned to the pirate/whale.

'I can only guess at what motivations led you to try and take the blame for that brute's actions, but it was a noble thing to do. Misguided though you were, I think that shows real strength of character. It may be that I have misjudged you whales after all.' And for the first time that any of the pirates had witnessed, Ahab cracked a smile. He patted the whale on the side of its gigantic face.

'In fact,' he continued, 'I'd like it very much if you'd be a guest at my home. I'm a famous curmudgeon, but underneath it all I'm really quite lonely, and it would be nice to have some company about the place.'

'Um. All right then,' said the pirate/whale.

Everybody cheered this happy outcome, and something of a carnival atmosphere broke out amongst the pirates. Ahab turned back to the Pirate Captain. He handed him a bulging bag of doubloons. 'Your reward, sir. You've earned it.'

The Pirate Captain looked at the doubloons wistfully for a moment, and then threw them over to Cutlass Liz. He watched the last bit of the *Lovely Emma* sink beneath the waves and heaved a forlorn sigh.

'Don't look so upset, Pirate Captain!' said Cutlass Liz, putting a consoling arm around his shoulder. 'You can always buy a new boat.'

The Pirate Captain shook his head. 'I haven't got so much as two pieces of eight to rub together.'

'You must have something?' said Cutlass Liz encouragingly.

'The ultimate treasure?'

'Is that one of those richer-in-spirit things about wet butterflies?'

'Something along those lines.'

'Not really my thing, I'm afraid. Come on, what's in those voluminous pockets of yours?'

The Pirate Captain emptied his pockets onto the top of a barrel. 'I've got a chocolate groat with fluff on it, a 'one child gets in free' voucher to see the lunatics at Bedlam, some seaweed, and an apple core. What kind of a boat can I get with that?'

'I think I've got just the thing,' said Cutlass Liz with a grin.

Fourteen

SHE LAUGHED HER WAY TO MURDER!

Later that night, back in the familiar if ramshackle surroundings of their old pirate boat, the pirates were all lying on deck looking at the stars.

'That constellation looks just like a tiny-headed horse who's swallowed a huge rectangle,' said the pirate in green.

'Rubbish. It looks like a beautiful mermaid lady,' said the sassy pirate.

'Oh, you think everything looks like a beautiful mermaid lady,' said the pirate with a scarf. The Pirate Captain stepped onto the deck wearing his dressing gown and smoking a postadventure cigar.

'Up late, lads,' he said, blowing a relaxed smoke ring. 'Don't forget—even us pirates need our beauty sleep.'

'Sorry, Captain. We were just discussing what that constellation looks like.' The pirate in green pointed at where they were looking. The Pirate Captain craned his neck and looked up.

'It looks just like my Prize Ham,' he said, a little sadly. The pirates all nodded in agreement.

'Sometimes I think there's nothing a good piece of ham can't do,' said the pirate with a scarf. 'The way that she bounced straight into the whale's blowhole. It was almost as if she were deliberately trying to sacrifice herself for you.'

'You mean like Baby Jesus?' asked the albino pirate, wide-eyed.

'I suppose so,' said the pirate with a scarf thoughtfully.

'Except Baby Jesus never had a delicious honey-roast glaze, did he? So in many ways my ham was a lot better than Baby Jesus ever was,' pointed out the Pirate Captain. He took off his pirate hat and lay down next to his crew.

'It's good to have the old boat back,' he said. 'I don't know why I ever let you lot talk me into getting a different one.'

'I'm glad there were too many barnacles on her for Cutlass Liz to chop her into firewood.'

'Good old barnacles.'

'I miss the *Lovely Emma*'s swimming pool though,' said the sassy pirate.

'And her panoramic views,' added the pirate in green.

'But I think we learnt a lot on this adventure, Pirate Captain,' said the scarf-wearing pirate, 'so it hasn't been a dead loss.'

'You're right,' said the Pirate Captain, closing his eyes and listening to the quiet rumble of the ocean. 'We learnt that getting into debt is not a matter to be taken lightly.'

'Also, we learnt that making an extravagant gesture to impress a girl is pretty stupid,' said the albino pirate.

'We tend to "learn" that on most adventures,' said the pirate with rickets.

'And most importantly of all we learnt the grass might look greener in showbusiness or whaling or something like that. But that when it comes down to it, you're often better off sticking with what you know,' said the pirate with a scarf.

'So long as what you know is kicking about the High Seas being a pirate, that is.'

'Oh yes, the lesson wouldn't apply if you had a regular job. In fact, anybody that did would be strongly advised to give it up right now and become a pirate themselves.'

With that the pirates went downstairs to do some shantying. And they were soon enjoying themselves so much that they barely even noticed when the pirate boat's mast fell down again.

LEARN MORE ABOUT . . .

Debt

Like the Pirate Captain, more people than ever are getting into serious debt, with the accompanying risks of depression, worry, and not being able to buy things that you want.

- If you're desperate about debt, call the National Debtline free on 0808 808 4000.
- The snappily titled Consumer Credit Counselling Service (www.cccs.co.uk) will help turn that debt frown upside down by talking about budgeting and that.

Remember—no matter how bad things seem, there's always a way out. Just look at the Pirate Captain—a whale attacked his boat and he was fine in the end!

Whale Conservation

The pirates' adventure was set in the olden days, when it was all right to go whaling. But nowadays things are different—there are thought to be around 570,000 sperm whales left in the sea, down from 2,000,000 in the 1940s. If you're concerned about whales (sperm or otherwise), you can help make a difference:

- Join the Whale and Dolphin Conservation Society (www.wdcs.org). You'll get a whale-tail sticker!
- If you see a stranded whale, call the British Divers Marine Life Rescue on 01825 765 546. If they're not in, try the RSPCA (08705 555 999) or Environment Agency (0800 807 060). *Don't* throw stuff at the stranded whale.
- Try to restrict your consumption of whale meat and ambergris to special occasions.

Nantucket

The pirates didn't get much of a chance to explore the historic town of Nantucket, but there's nothing to stop *you* from finding out more!

- The Nantucket Island Chamber of Commerce have loads of information about visiting the island, along with a low-resolution map and live weather updates. They also publish the official 288-page guidebook.
- The mission of the Nantucket Historical Association (www.nha.org) is to preserve the island's unique history and tell people about it. Pop to their website and have fun finding out more.
- Nantucket is also famous for its cranberry bogs. Why not pour yourself a cool glass of cranberry juice and sip it while thinking about harpoons?

ACKNOWLEDGEMENTS

Thanks to:

Rob Adey, Chloe Brown, Cilla McIntosh, Rodney Brown, Sam Brown, Matt Evans, Helen Garnons-Williams, Fiona Hankey, Yvonne Kee, David Murkin, Rebecca Murkin, Claire Paterson, and Brigid Way.

Don't forget to check out these other great titles in 'The Pirates!' series, all available at your local bookstore:

The Pirates! In an Adventure with Scientists
The Pirates! In an Adventure with Rasputin
The Pirates! In an Adventure with Americans
The Pirates! In an Adventure with Ice Cream
The Pirates! In an Adventure with Railroads
The Pirates! In an Adventure with the Green Ghost
The Pirates! In an Adventure with the Village of Fear
The Pirates! In an Adventure in Tir Na Nog
The Pirates! In an Adventure with Pigs
The Pirates! In an Adventure with Golems
The Pirates! In an Adventure with Rabbis
The Pirates! In an Adventure with Rabbits
The Pirates! In an Adventure with Mondays
The Seven Habits of Highly Effective Pirates
The Pirates! In an Adventure with Eskimos
The Pirates! In an Adventure with Cannibals
Watch Yourself, Pirate Captain!
The Pirates Get Sexy
The Pirates! In an Adventure with Space Pirates
Back to Pirate Academy, Pirate Captain!
Back to Pirate Academy 2, Pirate Captain!
Back to Pirate Academy 3, Pirate Captain!
Back to Pirate Academy 4, Pirate Captain!
Back to Pirate Academy 5, Pirate Captain!
Back to Pirate Academy 6, Pirate Captain!
Back to Pirate Academy 7, Pirate Captain!
The Pirates! In an Adventure with Murder
The Pirates! On Holiday
The Pirates! In an Adventure with the Stock Market
Pirate Captain and Son
The Pirates! In an Adventure with Lingerie
The Pirates Ride Out
The Pirates Go Ape
The Pirates! In an Adventure with Your Mother
The Pirates! In an Adventure with Freemasons

The Pirates! In an Adventure with Puppets
The Pirates! In an Adventure with Automatons
The Pirates! In an Adventure with Prussians
The Pirates! In an Adventure with Heavy Petting
I, Pirate Captain
The Pirates Go Fruit Picking
The Pirates! In an Adventure with a Very Windy Day
The Pirates! In an Adventure with Football
The Pirates and the Blacksmith's Daughter
The Pirates! In an Adventure with Gypsies
Ring a Ring of Pirates
Half a Pound of Tupenny Rice, Half a Pound of Pirates
The Pirates! In an Adventure with the Thieves of Time
The Pirates! In an Adventure with Haute Couture
The Pirates! In Two Hours 'Til Doomsday
Pirates Down the Rhine
The Pirates Make a Midnight Escape
The Ballad of the Pirate Captain
The Pirates! In an Adventure with a Secret
A Stitch in Time Saves Pirates
The Pirates Have Egyptian Capers
The Pirates! In an Adventure with the Triads
The Pirates! In an Adventure with the Pope
The Pirates! In an Adventure with Spring-Heel Jack
The Pirates' Underwater Adventure
The Pirates and the Citadel of Chaos
The Pirates! In an Adventure with the G.O.P.
The Pirates! In an Adventure with Tunnels
The Pirates' Holiday Special
The Pirate Treasury
The Pirates! In an Adventure with a Mysterious Gas
The Pirates! In an Adventure with Spectral Hands
The Pirates! In an Adventure with Mongol Hordes
The Pirates! In an Adventure with Spiders
Think Fast, Pirate Captain!
Black Bellamy Rides Again
Pirate vs. Pirate
The Pirates! In Mayhem Cove
The Pirates! In an Adventure with a Steep Hill
The Pirates Play Dead
The Pirates! In an Adventure with Nuts
The Pirates! In an Adventure with Wasps
You Can Do It, Pirate Captain!
The Pirates' Super T-shirts
The Pirates Sleep with the Lights On
The Pirates on Halloween
The Pirates Making It
The Pirates! In an Adventure with the Political Supremacy of the Bourgeoisie
The Pirates! In an Adventure with Risk Management
The Pirates! Commit a Series of Horrific Atrocities
The Pirates! In an Adventure with Geordies
Pirate Fever!

The Pirates and the Edge of Reason
The Pirates! In an Adventure with Public Sanitation
The Pirates! In an Adventure with Chess
The Pirates Strut Their Stuff
The Pirates! In an Adventure with an Ant
The Pirates! In an Adventure with a Harlequin
The Pirates! In an Adventure with a Damp Smell
The Pirates: Going Straight
The Pirates Embrace Diversity
P.I.R.A.T.E.
The Pirates Justify Themselves
The Pirates! In an Adventure with Gigolos
The Pirates! In an Adventure with Femmes Fatales
Jet Set Pirates!
The Moon's A Doubloon
The Pirates! In a Worker's Utopia
The Pirates! In an Adventure with Eugenics
Quite So, Pirate Captain
The Pirates! In an Adventure with the Alamo
The Pirates! In an Adventure with Rita, Sue & Bob Too
The Pirates! In an Adventure Down Mexico Way
The Pirates! In an Adventure with the Special Olympics
The Pirates! In an Adventure with Catastrophe Theory
The Pirates! In an Adventure with Slum Landlords
Konichiwa, Pirate Captain!
The Pirates! In an Adventure with Difference Engines
Bladderwrack!
The Cutlass and the Rose
The Pirates' Rainy Day Indoors
The Pirates! In an Adventure with Spies
Stone the Crows, Pirate Captain!
The Pirates Are Killing Music
Black Bellamy's Gambit
The Pirates! In an Adventure with Smugglers
The Pirates! Learn German in Five Easy Lessons
The Pirates! Shoot Horses with Cannons
This Little Pirate Went to Market
The Pirates! Run Amok
The Pirates! In an Adventure with the Jungle of Destiny
The Pirates! Fanny About on a Yacht
The Pirates! Remember the Olden Days
The Pirates! In an Adventure with the Jorvik Centre
The Pirates! In an Adventure with the Spelling Bee
The Pirates! In an Adventure with Disguises & Make-up
The Pirates! In an Adventure with Ponies & Riding
The Pirates! In an Adventure with Bikes
The Pirates! In an Adventure with Jennifer Garner
The Pirates! In an Adventure with the Goonies
The Pirates! In an Adventure with Foot & Mouth
The Pirates! In an Adventure with the Lubbock Lake Landmark
The Pirates! In an Adventure with Maths & Numbers
The Pirates! In an Adventure with Lola Montez

The Pirates! In an Adventure with the Kretzmer Syndrome
The Pirates! In an Adventure with the Honey Trap
The Pirates! In an Adventure with the Girls from Café Noir
The Pirates! In an Adventure with Skeletons
The Pirates! In an Adventure with Shaft
The Pirates Do Dallas
The Pirates! In an Adventure with Lazy Post-modernism
The Pirates! In an Adventure with Monkey's Delight
The Pirates! In an Adventure with a Spooky Eye
The Pirates! In an Adventure with Brockwell Infants School
The Pirates! In an Adventure That Goes Wrong
The Pirates! In an Adventure with the Circus of Death
The Pirates! In an Adventure with the Path of Least Resistance
The Pirates! In an Adventure with the Empire State Human
The Pirates! In an Adventure with the Dignity of Labour (Parts 1–4)
The Pirates Colouring-in Book
The Pirates! In an Adventure with the Culture of Fear
The Pirates! Build a Base in the Woods
The Pirates! In an Adventure with Unshaven Men
The Pirates! Have Been Running with Scissors Again
The Pirates! In an Adventure with the Red Hand Gang
The Pirates! In an Adventure with the IRS
The Pirates! In an Adventure with That Man on Beta
The Pirates! In an Adventure with the Bronze Girls of the Shaolin
The Pirates! In a Big Top Adventure
The Pirates! In an Adventure with Jazzy Jeff
The Pirates! In an Adventure with Boggle
The Pirates! In an Adventure with Richard Dawkins
The Pirates! Together in Electric Dreams
You've Got to Fight for Your Right to Pirate
The Pirates! In an Adventure with the Cartesian Theatre
Leave It to Pirates
The Pirates! And the Mystery of the Stuttering Parrot
The Pirates! And the Secret of Phantom Lake
The Pirates! In an Adventure in Idaho
The Pirates! In an Adventure with Mormons
Oy Vey, Pirate Captain!
A Very Peculiar Pirate
The Pirates! Did Not Mean to Say That Out Loud
The Pirates! In an Adventure with Zombies
The Pirates! In an Adventure with Cowboys
The Pirates! In an Adventure with Richard Nixon
Don't Stop Now, Pirate Captain!
The Pirates and the Phenomenological Garden
The Pirates! In an Adventure Down the Anchor
The Pirates! Are Overdoing It a Bit

Join the **Captain's Cutlass Club** and receive a free **Pirate Badge.** This attractive three-colour badge, pinned to your blazer lapel or jumper, will excite the interest and comment of all your friends! Send a self-addressed envelope to **Orion House, 5 Upper Saint Martin's Lane, London, WC2H 9EA (UK).**

USES FOR PHYSET
Nowadays
most of us only tend to eat a tiny fraction of the COMMON SPERM WHALE, but in the C19th people managed to find a use for every single part of the whale's anatomy.
RIBS
Used to
prod chimne
sweeps free.
TAIL
The Palace of Westminster is built mainly from Whale tails.
GUTS
Made into
skipping rop
for schoolgirl
WHALE SKIN
Spats for the poor.
HEART
Cut in half make
a fashionable hear
bonnet

Gideon Defoe

THE PIRATES! In an Adventure with Scientists

Not since *Moby-Dick*. . . . No, not since *Treasure Island*. . . . Actually, not since Jonah and the Whale has there been a sea saga to rival *The Pirates! In an Adventure with Scientists,* featuring the greatest seafaring hero of all time, the immortal Pirate Captain, who, although he lives for months at a time at sea, somehow manages to keep his beard silky and in good condition.

Worried that his pirates are growing bored with a life of winking at pretty native ladies and trying to stick enough jellyfish together to make a bouncy castle, the Pirate Captain decides it's high time to spearhead an adventure.

While searching for some major pirate booty, he mistakenly attacks the young Charles Darwin's *Beagle* and then leads his ragtag crew from the exotic Galapagos Islands to the fog-filled streets of Victorian London. There they encounter grisly murder, vanishing ladies, radioactive elephants, and the Holy Ghost itself. And that's not even the half of it.

Gideon Defoe, who lives in London, is also the author of *The Pirates! In an Adventure with Ahab* and the forthcoming *The Pirates! In an Adventure with Communists* (Pantheon Books, 2006). His mother does not regard writing stupid books about pirates as any kind of an occupation for an adult.

Flip this book for *The Pirates! In an Adventure with Ahab* . . .

A Note

Hello Lubbers!

Here is a map of our exciting adventure with scientists. You are probably looking at it and thinking "WOW! that map is so good and accurate the Pirate Captain must have traced it!" You would be wrong I drew it freehand even the difficult bits like Scotland. I got bored with the cross-hatching so I let the Albino Pirate do most of that but the rest is all 100% me.

Yours
The Pirate Captain

THE FALKLA

YOU ARE HERE

THE PIRATES IN AN ADVENTURE WITH COWBOYS

THE WEST INDIES

SKULL Island

Scale: 3×Double Decker Bus

The HIGH SEAS

Chesterfield

LONDON

LITTLEHAMPTON

THE GALAPAGOS ISLANDS

DS '03

ALSO BY GIDEON DEFOE

The Pirates! In an Adventure with Ahab

THE PIRATES!

In an Adventure with Scientists

THE PIRATES!

In an Adventure with Scientists

Gideon Defoe

Vintage Books
A Division of Random House, Inc.
NEW YORK

FIRST VINTAGE BOOKS EDITION, JULY 2006

The Library of Congress has cataloged the Pantheon edition as follows:
Defoe, Gideon.
The pirates! : in an adventure with scientists / Gideon Defoe.
p. cm.
1. Darwin, Charles, 1809–1882—Fiction. 2. *Beagle* (Ship)—Fiction. 3. Scientists—Fiction. 4. Pirates—Fiction. I. Title: Pirates! in an adventure with scientists.
II. Title.
PR6104.E525P57 2004
823'.92—dc22
2004044570

Vintage ISBN-10: 1-4000-7750-8
Vintage ISBN-13: 978-1-4000-7750-2

www.vintagebooks.com
www.gideondefoe.com

Printed in the United States of America
10 9 8 7 6 5 4 3 2

To Sophie,
who has a quarter of a million pounds

CONTENTS

THE PIRATES!

In an Adventure with Scientists

One

INTO ACTION UNDER THE PIRATE FLAG!

'The best bit about being a pirate,' said the pirate with gout, 'is the looting.'

'That's rubbish!' said the albino pirate. 'It's the doubloons. Doubloons are easily the best bit about pirating.'

The rest of the pirates, sunning themselves on the deck of the pirate boat, soon joined in. It had been several weeks since the Pirates' Adventure with Cowboys, and they had a lot of time on their hands.

'It's the pirate grog!'

'Marooning! That's what I like best!'

'Cutlasses!'

'The Spanish Main!'

'The ship's biscuits!'

One of the pirates pulled a special face to show exactly what he thought of this last comment, and soon all the pirates were fighting. With a sound like a bat hitting a watermelon, pirate fist connected with pirate jaw and a gold tooth bounced across the deck. The pirate with gout found himself run through in a grisly manner, and one of the cabin boys accidentally got a shiny pirate hook in the

side of the head. It would probably have gone on for hours in this fashion, but both of the heavy wooden doors that led to the downstairs of the boat crashed open, and out onto the deck strode the Pirate Captain himself.

The Pirate Captain cut an impressive figure. If you were to compare him to a type of tree—and working out what sort of tree they would be if they were trees instead of pirates was easily one of the crew's favourite pastimes—he would undoubtedly be an oak, or maybe a horse chestnut. He was all teeth and curls, but with a pleasant, open face; his coat was of a better cut than everybody else's, and his beard was fantastic and glossy, and the ends of it were twisted with expensive-looking ribbons. Living at sea tended to leave you with ratty, matted hair, but the Pirate Captain somehow kept his beard silky and in good condition, and though nobody knew his secret, they all respected him for it. They also respected him because it was said he was wedded to the sea. A lot of pirates claimed that they were wedded to the sea, but usually this was an excuse because they couldn't get a girlfriend or they were gay pirates, but in the Pirate Captain's case none of his crew doubted he was actually wedded to the sea for a minute. Any of his men would have gladly taken a bullet for him, or even the pointy end of a cutlass. The Pirate Captain didn't need to do much more than clear his throat and roll his eyes a bit to stop the fighting dead in its tracks.

'What's going on, you scurvy knaves!' he bellowed. Pirates were often rude to each other, but without really meaning it, so none of the brawling pirates took being called a 'scurvy knave' too much to heart.

'We were just discussing what the best bit about being a pirate is,' answered the pirate dressed in green, after a bit of an awkward pause.

'The best bit about being a pirate?'

'Yes sir. We couldn't quite decide. I mean, it's all good . . .'

'The best bit about being a pirate is the shanties.'

And with the argument settled, the Pirate Captain strode back into the galley, indicating for the pirate with a scarf to follow. The rest of the crew were left on their own.

'He's right. It's the shanties,' said the albino pirate thoughtfully. One of the other pirates nodded.

'They *are* really good. Shall we sing a pirate shanty?'

The Pirate Captain was secretly relieved when he heard the strains of a rowdy shanty coming through the roof of the galley. Just recently he had been worrying about discipline on board the pirate boat, and there was an old pirate motto: If the men are singing a shanty, then they can't be up to mischief.*

'Come into my office for a moment,' he told the pirate with a scarf, who was his trusty second in command. The Pirate Captain's office was full of mementoes from the previous pirate adventures. There was a ten-gallon hat from the Pirates' Adventure with Cowboys, and some old bits of tentacle from the Pirates' Adventure with Squid, as well as several Post-it Notes reminding the Pirate Captain to say things like 'Splice the mainsail!' or 'Hard about, lads!' On the walls there hung several fantastic paintings of the Pirate Captain himself—one of them showed him looking anguished and cradling a dead swan: this painting was titled *WHY?* Another was of the Pirate Captain reclining naked except for a small piece of gauze. And a third pictured the Pirate Captain sharing a strange futuristic-looking drink with a lady who seemed to be made from metal. There were also quite a lot of nautical maps and charts about the place, and even an astrolabe. The Pirate Captain wasn't 100 per cent sure what the astrolabe did, or whether it was actually an astrolabe rather than a sextant, but he enjoyed fiddling with it when he got

*'Shanty' probably derives from the French word *chanter*, meaning 'to sing.' Most shanties tended to be about frisky mermaids who loved putting out for sailors more than anyone.

bored, nonetheless. Right at the moment boredom was an issue that weighed heavily on the Pirate Captain's mind.

'Care for some grog?' he asked politely. The scarf-wearing pirate wasn't very thirsty, but he said yes anyway, because if you start turning down grog when you're a pirate it doesn't help your reputation much.

'Ship's biscuits? I've got ship's custard creams, and ship's bourbons,' said the Pirate Captain. He held out a tin that had a boat painted on it and the pirate with a scarf took a bourbon, because he knew custard creams were the Pirate Captain's favourites.

'What do you think all that brawling was about, number two?' asked the Pirate Captain, absentmindedly seeing how fast he could spin the astrolabe using just one finger.

'Like the men said . . . it was just a friendly discussion that got a bit out of hand,' replied the scarf-wearing pirate, not entirely sure where the Pirate Captain was going with this, but amazed as always that he could carry on a conversation whilst doing complex calculations with an astrolabe. That sort of thing was why the Pirate Captain was the Pirate Captain, the pirate with a scarf reflected.

'I'll tell you what it was about,' said the Pirate Captain. 'It was about bored pirates! I've made a mistake. We've been moored here in . . . in the . . .' The Pirate Captain rubbed his nose, which he liked to think of as a stentorian nose, even though stentorian is actually a tone of voice, and squinted at one of the charts.

'The West Indies, sir,' said the scarf-wearing pirate, helpfully.

'Mmmm. Well, we've been here too long. I thought that after our exciting adventure with those cowboys, we could all do with a break, but I guess us pirates are only really happy when we're pirating.'

'I think you're right, sir,' the scarf-wearing pirate said. 'It's nice enough here, but I keep on finding sand in my grog, from all that lying about on the beach. And those native women, wandering about with no tops on . . . it's a bit much.'

'Exactly. It's time we had another pirate adventure!'

'I'll let the other pirates know. Where will we be heading for? Skull Island? The Spanish Main?'

'Oh, Lord, no! If we plunder the Spanish Main* one more time, I think I'll tear out my own beard,' said the Pirate Captain, trying on the ten-gallon hat and narrowing his eyes like a cowboy as he studied his reflection in the mirror.

'So what were you thinking?'

'Something will come up. It usually does. Just make sure we've got plenty of hams on board. I didn't really enjoy our last adventure much, because we ran out of hams about halfway through. And what's my motto? "I like ham!" '

'It's a good motto, sir.'

Back on deck, the other pirates had finished their shanty—which had been about how a beautiful sea-nymph had left her rich but stupid Royal Navy boyfriend for a pirate boyfriend because he was much more interesting to talk to and could make her laugh—and now they were roaring. This was another common pastime amongst the pirates.

'Rah!'

'Oooh-arg!'

'Aaaarrrr, me hearties!'

It didn't mean much, but it filled a few hours. They all stopped when they saw the pirate with a scarf had come back from his meeting with the Pirate Captain. He almost slipped in a pool of the cabin boy's blood that was left over from the fight.

'Can somebody swab these decks?' he said, a little tetchily. Left to their own devices, the pirates tended towards the bone idle.

'It's Tuesday! Sunday is boat cleaning day!'

'I know, but somebody could get hurt.'

The diffident pirate gave a shrug and went off to find a swabbing cloth, whilst the remaining crew looked up expectantly from where

*It was Francis Drake who had first made the Spanish Main a popular target, back in 1571. A replica of his boat, the *Golden Hind*, can be found today next to London Bridge.

they were sprawled. The scarf-wearing pirate gazed out across the sparkling water, and at the tropical beach with its alabaster sands, and the forest of coconut palms behind that, and then he noticed one of the pretty native ladies and so he quickly looked back down at his pirate shoes.

'Listen up, pirates,' he said. 'I know all this endless wandering up and down the beach . . . and our interminable attempts at trying to choose which sort of mouth-watering exotic fruit to eat . . . and all these wanton tropical girls knocking around . . . I know it's been getting you down.'

A couple of the pirates muttered something to each other, but the scarf-wearing pirate didn't quite catch what they said.

'So you'll be happy to know,' he went on, 'that the Pirate Captain has ordered us to put to sea, just as soon as we've collected some hams for the journey.'

A buzz of excitement ran around the deck.

'Perhaps we should cook the hams first, before setting off?' asked the pirate dressed in green.

'That sounds like a good idea,' said the albino pirate.

'Do you think roasting is best?' asked the pirate with a nut allergy.

The scarf-wearing pirate sighed, because he knew how seriously the pirates took their ham, and he could predict how this was going to end up. He tried to look hard-nosed, which involved tensing all the muscles in his nostrils, and with as much authority as he could manage he said, 'Yes, roasting is good. It allows the free escape of watery particles that's necessary for a full flavour. But we've got to make sure it's regulated by frequent basting with the fat that has exuded from the meat, combined with a little salt and water—otherwise the hams will burn, and become hard and tasteless.'

'Roasting?* Are you sure?' asked the surly pirate who was dressed in red, barely concealing his contempt. 'What about boil-

*In those days, roasting would have meant spit-roasting. A popular craze in the early part of the nineteenth century was to use a small dog fastened to a treadmill to turn the spit, freeing up the cook to prepare other dishes.

ing? I always find a boiled ham becomes more savoury in taste and smell, and more firm and digestible.'

'Ah, but if you continue the process too long, you risk the hams becoming tough and less succulent,' said the pirate in green.

'But the loss from roasting is upwards of twenty-two per cent of the ham! The loss from boiling is only about sixteen per cent. More ham for us! That can only be a good thing.'

'We need to dust the hams with bread raspings if we're going to boil them. And we should dress the knuckle bone with a frill of white paper.'

'A frill of white paper? What kind of a pirate are you? Rah!'

The pirates started to fight again, and it wasn't until one of them noticed that the Pirate Captain had come back from his cabin and was now leaning against the mast, drumming his fingers on a barrel, that they shuffled to attention.

'That's enough of that, my beauties!' he roared. 'Let's set a course'—at this point the Pirate Captain paused in what he hoped would be a dramatic and exciting fashion—'for adventure!'

The crew just gave him a bit of a collective blank look. The Pirate Captain sighed.

'All right,' he said with a pout, 'south.'

Two

RETURN TO SKULL ISLAND!

'That was some hurricane!' said the pirate who was prone to exaggeration, emptying the seawater that had collected in his pirate boots over the side of the boat. 'I don't think I've ever seen one like it! I thought the mast was going to crack for sure! And we must have lost half a dozen men, just washed away into the deep.'*

'That wasn't a hurricane. It wasn't even a storm,' said the pirate in red.

'Well, gale then. That was some gale.'

'Pfft!' said the pirate in red. He was fed up, because a whole day had gone by and they didn't seem to be any closer to actually starting an adventure.

'According to my Beaufort Scale,' said the albino pirate, waving a nautical pamphlet at the rest of the crew, 'a hurricane is number twelve, or "that which no canvas could withstand." As you can see, our canvases are fine, so it obviously wasn't a hurricane. I should say it was somewhere between number six, a Strong Breeze—or

*The Caribbean and the Gulf of Mexico were, and are, subject to devastating hurricanes. In 1712 Governor Hamilton reported that a storm had destroyed thirty-eight ships in the harbour at Port Royal and nine ships at Kingston.

"that which will send a pirate's hat flying and muss up his luxuriant beard"—and number eight, a Fresh Gale—or "that which will make a pirate's trousers billow about so that it looks like he has fat legs".'

'Are you sure that's an actual Beaufort Scale you've got there?' asked the scarf-wearing pirate.

'Of course I'm sure,' snapped the albino pirate. 'The Pirate Captain wrote it out for me himself.'

All the pirates were too tired even to roar at each other, let alone sing a shanty, after their strenuous efforts in bringing the boat through the previous night's fantastic storm or fresh gale or strong breeze or whatever it happened to be. So they just sprawled on the deck, looking up at the last few seagulls to have made it this far out from land, circling above in what was now a clear blue sky. It wasn't until the smell of fresh ham wafted from the boat's kitchen that the pirates stirred and went below to the pirate dining room.

The Pirate Captain was already sitting at the table, tapping his knife and fork expectantly. Of all the pirates, it was true that nobody loved his ham more than the Pirate Captain. The hams were brought to the table, and they had been roasted, which annoyed the pirate who had argued they should have been boiled, but he was so hungry he didn't bother to complain, and he had to admit that they tasted delicious. The pirates tore into their food and grog with the relish that comes from a hard night's pirating.

'Honestly, pirates! Have you forgotten that you are provided with teeth? Small wonder you complain about indigestion when you forget to chew!' admonished the Pirate Captain.

'I thought it was cold feet that gave you indigestion,' said the pirate with a hook where his hand should have been. 'And that wrapping your feet in a hot towel would prevent such belly pains.'

'That's headaches, idiot!' said the pirate in green.

'No. Headaches are most commonly caused from reading by candlelight, when the candle is positioned incorrectly. It should be

placed behind you, so the rays can pass directly over your shoulder to the book.'

The pirates almost started fighting again over this, but the Pirate Captain held up an imperious hand and started to speak.

'I got a letter this morning,' he said, 'from our old enemy Black Bellamy.'

The pirates muttered a few oaths. Black Bellamy was the roguish rival pirate whom the pirates had encountered during the Pirates' Adventure with Buried Treasure and the Pirates' Adventure with the Princess of Cadiz. Somehow they weren't surprised that they had not heard the last of him.

'Black Bellamy has invited us to a feast on board his schooner, the *Barbary Hen,* which is sailing just a few leagues from here.'

'It's Black Bellamy, Captain! You can't mean to trust him!' said the albino pirate. The other pirates nodded.

'Perhaps he's changed,' said the Pirate Captain. 'He says in his letter that he's changed, and that he wants to hold this feast to make up for all the trouble he and his villainous crew have caused us in the past.'

'Oh, well. You can't really argue with that sort of sentiment,' agreed the pirate in green.

'Yes, that seems really nice of him,' said the albino pirate, feeling a bit guilty for being so harsh on Black Bellamy just a few seconds ago.

'And it would be good to see how they prepare their hams on board the *Barbary Hen,*' added the pirate in red.

'So it's settled. We'll accept the invitation and set sail for Black Bellamy's feast at once!' said the Pirate Captain, picking a piece of ham from his immaculate beard.

The moonlit waters were clear and calm as the pirate boat moored up alongside the *Barbary Hen*. The pirate crew piled into a launch—

'Shotgun!' shouted the sassy pirate who liked to sit up front with the Captain—and paddled across to where a rope-ladder had been hung over the other ship's side. There were around forty head of hog wandering about the darkened decks, which was clearly Black Bellamy's way of impressing his guests. Black Bellamy politely took the pirates' coats and cutlasses. This showed he really *had* changed, because the Black Bellamy of old was famous for his lack of manners. But he was still a fearsome sight, with a beard that came up to his eyes, two pairs of pistols hanging at the end of a silk sling, and a big knife held between his teeth.

'Herro. Relcon ahord ha *Harrarry Hen,*' said Black Bellamy.

'What did he say?' whispered the pirate in green.

'I think he said, "Welcome aboard the *Barbary Hen.*" It's a bit hard to tell, because of that knife clenched between his teeth,' said the scarf-wearing pirate.

Black Bellamy made a few incomprehensible introductions, and then led the pirates into his feasting hall. Their old rival had certainly pulled out all the stops—there was roast veal, which had half a pint of melted butter poured over it, fillets of beef garnished with slices of lemon, a sumptuous pork broth, potato scones, stewed mushrooms . . . several of the pirates had to use their pirate neckerchiefs to wipe saliva from their mouths. It didn't matter that they had already eaten a sumptuous feast earlier that day, because they often had adventures comprised of nothing but sumptuous feasts. Initially, because there was so much history between them, the two sets of pirates were a bit hostile, and conversation was understandably awkward, but after some pirate grog they were soon carousing with each other. Piratical conversation buzzed about the boat.

'Diving. Have you ever tried it? It's fantastic! We went and dived at the wreck of an actual pirate ship!'

'My friend here thinks you should boil hams, but he's an idiot.'

'. . . 'twas the unmistakable tang of human flesh . . .'

'. . . and I'm not making this up—he had a wooden leg!'

Both Black Bellamy and the Pirate Captain were pleased it was going so well.

'Why don't we adjourn to my drawing room, for a spot of cards?* Hmmm?' said Black Bellamy to the Pirate Captain. The Pirate Captain could have gone on eating mutton necks all night, but his host had been so gracious he thought it rude to refuse.

The pirates were a bit annoyed by how nice the drawing room was, especially when Black Bellamy flipped open the top of a huge mahogany globe to reveal a little drinks cabinet. The Pirate Captain's globe back on board the pirate boat was made out of tin and about the size of a football, and he wasn't even sure it had Africa on it, so it was difficult not to feel a pang of jealousy. Black Bellamy poured out some rum from a crystal decanter and suggested a game of Cincinnati High Low.

'Oh, that's a lucky man's game,' said the Pirate Captain, because he had heard someone say this before.

'Well, what would you suggest?' asked Black Bellamy amiably. 'Crossfire? Seven Card Flip? Mexican Seven Card Stud?'

He was just showing off, thought the Pirate Captain, but he was no slouch at cards himself.

'How about,' said the Pirate Captain, 'Cat's Cradle? Or Round the World? Or Walking the Dog?'

'Those are yo-yo tricks.'

'Ha! Of course they are. Well then, that one with the Mexicans.'

They settled down to the card game. Pretty soon the Pirate Captain was down several doubloons, and pretty soon after that he had lost all the boat's precious supply of hams. The trouble was that Black Bellamy's beard, coming up all the way to his eyes as it did,

*Captain Johnson's *General History of the Pyrates* tells us that most pirate ships had a set of Articles, by which the crew had to adhere. Article 3 states, 'No person to game at cards or dice for money', so Black Bellamy is showing his maverick colours here.

gave him a perfect poker face. The Pirate Captain's crew was starting to get worried, but then the Pirate Captain had a fantastic idea. He found himself with another useless hand but this time, instead of thumping the table and looking miserable, he gave a big grin, and whispered loudly to the pirate who wore a scarf, 'We'll be feasting on that forty head of hog, with this brilliant hand!'

Black Bellamy heard this, and decided to fold. The Pirate Captain shuffled the pile of doubloons into his pockets. Black Bellamy saw his cards and gasped.

'But . . . you had a terrible hand! Garbage!'

'Yes. But I knew that if I looked pleased with it, you would think it was a flush or something like that!'

'You're confounded clever!' roared Black Bellamy. 'But listen. Give me back all those doubloons I've just lost, and in return I'll tell you where you can find ten times that sort of loot.'

The Pirate Captain thought about Black Bellamy's offer for a second or two. Mathematics wasn't his strong point—obviously pirating was his strong point—but you didn't need to be Archimedes to realise that ten times the amount of doubloons he had just won was a good deal of cash.

'Very well, Black Bellamy,' said the Pirate Captain, taking the coins back out of his pockets. 'Where can we find this treasure?'

'I'll need to show you on the nautical charts,' sighed Black Bellamy, doing a sad face. 'Me and my men had been planning to sail to the South Seas, near the Galápagos Islands, where a ship belonging to the—uh—Bank of England is right this moment transporting . . . ooh, at least a hundred weight in gold bullion, back from the colonies. I'd been really looking forward to a spot of plundering, but I guess I'll just have to let you set about the raid yourself!'

'You're sure about this?' said the Pirate Captain, his eyes narrowing. 'That's eight hundred leagues from here. It's a little out of our way.'

'I swear by the Pirate Code.'

'Do you know the name of this ship?'

'It's called the *Beagle*. And it's chock full of gold, mark my words. Can I have those doubloons back now?'

As the pirates crossed back to their boat they could hear laughter coming from the *Barbary Hen*—it was good, thought the Pirate Captain, that they had left their hosts in such high spirits, even though he had got the better of Black Bellamy. And now he was pretty confident that they really *were* setting course . . . for adventure!

Though he didn't bother saying it out loud this time.

Three

PIRATE ISLANDS AND BLACK-HEARTED MEN!

'So, there's two pirate boats sailing towards each other,' said the short pirate with thick black spectacles, 'and one of the boats is carrying all this blue paint. And the other pirate boat is carrying all this red paint. They crash, and you know what happened?'

'What happened?'

'They were marooned! Ha-ha! You see?'

The pirates had started telling each other jokes in an attempt to ward off the inevitable boredom between feasts, because there wasn't much else to do on board a pirate boat. They had been at sea for a couple of days now, searching high and low for the *Beagle*. When the boat had first reached the tropical waters surrounding the Galápagos Islands the pirates kept themselves amused by capturing a couple of the giant turtles that frequented this part of the world, and then racing them about the deck.* You could fit two whole pirates on each shell. They constructed an obstacle course from bits of old rope and rigging, but the turtles proved a lot less resilient than they had hoped. A few of the pirates then had the bright idea

*Nowadays Galápagos Giant Turtles often accidentally eat plastic bags left as litter by unthinking tourists, mistaking them for tasty jellyfish.

that if they caught enough of the huge diaphanous jellyfish that circled about the boat, they could construct a kind of bouncy castle. This kept them occupied for a few more hours, but it didn't really work, and eventually they got tired of it, and found that they had jellyfish guts stuck all over their pirate boots.

The pirate dressed in green went downstairs to get a glass of water because he was nervous and his throat was dry. There was a note stuck next to the ship's sink, written in the Pirate Captain's familiar bubble writing. It read:

Will whoever keeps taking my mug STOP IT. *It is very annoying. Have a little respect for other people's property.*

The Pirate Captain

Life at sea was tough and unforgiving, and tensions could run quite high on board a pirate boat, especially when crockery was limited and people didn't always do their washing-up, but generally the pirates all got along fine. The pirate dressed in green gulped down the tap water—it was much nicer than seawater—and tried to pluck up courage for the task ahead. He'd been putting it off for ages, but now seemed as good a time as any.

There was a knock at the Pirate Captain's door, and then the pirate in green came in.

'Sorry to be bothering you, Captain,' he said. The Pirate Captain looked up. He had a lot to sort out in preparation for their imminent and audacious attack, but he made a point of always having time for the men.

'What can I do for you . . . uh . . . my fellow?' said the Pirate Captain, who often found it difficult to tell his crew apart from one another. 'Grog? Ham?'

'No thanks, sir. I was wondering if I could ask you something?'

'It's what I'm here for. You don't mind if I help myself?' said the Pirate Captain, indicating the slices of ham. 'Now, what is it?'

'Well, I was thinking of getting a tattoo.'

'They're quite popular.'

'Yes, Captain.'

'But they don't come off, you know.'

'Yes, Captain. I've thought about that.'

'Well then.'

'I thought it might be good to get a Skull and Crossbones, like we have on our flag, but it turns out a couple of the men have already got that. So . . . I was wondering . . . that's to say . . . would you have any objections . . .'

'Spit it out, man!'

'. . . if I got your face done instead? I was thinking of adding a little speech bubble, with—ha—you saying "Scurvy knaves!" like you always do. It would be on my arm, if that's all right.' He indicated the patch on his upper arm where he was going to have the tattoo.

For a moment, the Pirate Captain was speechless. The ham on his fork just hung in mid air.

'Of course . . . I . . . ah . . . I don't know what to say,' he said.

'Are you okay, Captain?'

'Yes . . . it's just this, um, ham. It's very spicy, and it's making my eyes water.'

In all their many adventures, even the one where they had battled zombie pirates, the Pirate Captain had never been so touched by a gesture from any of his loyal pirate crew. His lip began to tremble, and the pirate in green was mightily relieved when at that point the pirate with an accordion, breathless with excitement, hurried into the Captain's office.

'Sorry to interrupt, Captain, but we've caught sight of a ship, and we think it's the *Beagle,* because it has a funny-looking dog painted on the side. Should I get the men ready for boarding?'

The Pirate Captain swiftly regained his composure, and started

to bark out orders. 'Get the cannons ready first, and remind the pirates not to stand right behind them this time,' he bellowed. The Pirate Captain had explained basic Newtonian physics and the principles of recoil to his men more times than he could remember, but it just didn't seem to go in.

'And I want to hear plenty of roaring until we've secured the enemy vessel,' he said, picking up a telescope and marching onto the deck, where several of the pirates were already gathered.

'It's just a ten-gun brig,' said the scarf-wearing pirate, scratching thoughtfully at a livid scar that ran the length of his cheek. On most people a scar can be quite disfiguring, but several of the pirates thought that in the pirate with a scarf's case it actually added to his rather rugged appeal.

'A ten-gun brig? Really?' said the Pirate Captain, frowning at the news.

'I was expecting something bigger, seeing as it's carrying all this gold for the Bank of England,' said his number two.

'Perhaps they're trying to keep a low profile,' said the Pirate Captain, with some misgivings. 'Are those cannons ready?'

'This sort of makes us bank robbers, doesn't it?'

'Aaarrr. But you knew you'd be bending a few laws when you became a pirate. I'm not sure the ivory smuggling we were doing the other week was entirely respectable. Or all that trawling for cod, come to think about it.'

'Cannons ready, Captain.'

An eerie silence suddenly becalmed the pirate chatter, as the crew waited for the Pirate Captain to give his order to make good the attack.

'Fire a cannonball at that boat!' said the Pirate Captain.

Four

WHAT EVIL LURKS IN THE UNFORGIVING DEEP?

'Confound it, man!' said Robert FitzRoy, captain of the boat about to be attacked by the pirates. 'I told you women and the sea were a mighty bad combination.'

FitzRoy was young for a ship's captain, just twenty-seven, but the man he stood back-to-back with was younger still, a full five years his junior. Yet neither bore the frisky demeanour that you would expect to find in people under thirty.

'I can't help myself, Robert,' said his companion, Charles Darwin, cradling his big round head in his hands. 'I love her, and I mean to marry her!'

'But I love her too!' said FitzRoy. 'She drives me to distraction! You already knew that.'

'Damn women, with . . . with their hair . . . and their faces . . . ,' muttered Darwin.

'I must demand satisfaction,' said Captain FitzRoy. 'You don't leave me any choice.'

The cabin was a little small for a duel, neither man quite being able to stand up properly without grazing his head, but needs must at sea.

'Three years' voyage . . . and it should come to this,' said Darwin, shakily pouring powder into his pistol. 'May the best man win.'

'You're a botanist.* I'm a trained naval officer. I don't fancy your chances much,' said FitzRoy.

The door was flung open with a crash that made Darwin wince, and in ran the breathless cause of the two men's argument, the lovely Lady Mara. 'Please stop!' she said with her lovely mouth. 'There's—'

But before Lady Mara could say any more, a cannonball splintered through the cabin wall at tremendous speed, and buried itself in the side of her pretty head, knocking her off her feet, and leaving her quite dead on the floor. Darwin and FitzRoy stood, dumbfounded.

'Well. I . . .'

'Should we . . . ?' Darwin gestured at his gun.

'Hardly seems much point.'

'What a damned fool I've been!' laughed Darwin.

'Oh, I'm just as much to blame,' said FitzRoy with a grin, pocketing his pistol, and slapping his friend on the back. They would have hugged right there and then, but were interrupted by a further crash as first another cannonball and then a pirate screamed in through the window. The two men stood stock-still.

'Don't make any sudden movements,' whispered FitzRoy to his companion. 'Remember—he's more scared of us than we are of him.'

'That's bears, you idiot,' hissed Darwin out of the side of his mouth. 'I don't think it applies to pirates.'

*Darwin was serving as an unpaid naturalist on board the HMS *Beagle*. The *Beagle* was unimpressive for its day—just ninety feet long and of a notoriously unseaworthy design. In his notes Darwin described the voyage as 'one continual puke'.

At the doorway, a second pirate appeared, with a luxuriant beard and a pleasant, open face, all teeth and curls.

'I'm the Pirate Captain. And I'm here for the gold!' he said.

Everybody froze. For a moment the only sound was the gentle roar of the ocean, and some wheezing from the pirate with asthma.

'Well, uh, help yourself,' said FitzRoy eventually, slightly perplexed. Darwin was too terrified to speak.

'Not that there's a great deal,' continued the young captain. 'I think some of the portholes might be made of gold, but then again they could be made of brass. Same sort of colour, so it's difficult to tell.'

'Rah!' said the Pirate Captain, with a frightful bellow. 'I know you're carrying a hundred weight in gold bullion!'

'Really?' said FitzRoy, genuinely surprised. 'I haven't seen anything of the sort.'

'Perhaps the bit of boat that's under the water is made of gold,' ventured Darwin, finding his voice at last. 'I mean, it could be made of anything for all we know. You never get to see it.'

The Pirate Captain's icy blade against his throat struck him silent.

'Search the hold, men, and bring me back some gold,' said the Pirate Captain, with a sneer reminiscent of Elvis.

The pirates were pretty slick by this stage of their piratical careers, and they had managed to overrun the entire ship in a matter of minutes. The only casualty on the pirate side had been the pirate dressed in red, who had twisted his ankle trying to do that trick where you slide down the face of the mainsail, cutting it as you go with your cutlass—which worked fine up to a point but still left a twenty-foot drop once he reached the bottom of the canvas.

'Ouch! My ankle!' he cried, but none of the other pirates had much sympathy for his reckless showboating. A group of them headed into the hold—but instead of the clinking you would associate with gold, all they could hear was the chatter of creatures. One of

the pirates tore at a tarpaulin, only to discover row upon row of cages, each containing some sort of monkey.

'The gold must be hidden inside these monkeys!' shouted a pirate. Several of the pirates put down their flickering lamps, picked up monkeys of various different types, and slit them end to end, but all that spilt out was monkey guts.

'Gold!' said the pirate with an accordion, holding something yellowish up hopefully.

'That's not gold. It's a gall bladder,' said the pirate with a hook for his hand.

Covered in bits of creature, and thoroughly dejected, the pirate crew tramped back to FitzRoy's cabin.

'Pieces of ape! Pieces of ape!' squawked Gary, the ship's parrot.

'Will somebody shut him up?' scowled the pirate in green.

'There's no treasure here, Captain. Just a lot of stupid creatures,' said the pirate with a scarf.

'Just like I told you,' said FitzRoy.

The Pirate Captain sat down and rubbed his eyes with a weary hand. It suddenly felt like it had been a very long day.

'But Black Bellamy . . . he said you were carrying gold for the Bank of England.'

'The Bank of England?' said FitzRoy, grabbing at a table as the *Beagle* started to list alarmingly. 'I believe I've heard there is such a boat. But it's sailing in the vicinity of the West Indies, from what I remember.'

'The West Indies? But that's where we've just come from!'

'That Black Bellamy!' said the pirate with a hook instead of a hand. 'He was just trying to get us out of the way, so that he could plunder it for himself! Why, he hasn't changed at all! We've been bamboozled!'

The pirates were all very disappointed with the way Black Bellamy had behaved.

'So, then. Um. What are you doing in these parts?' said the Pirate Captain to Darwin, trying to make a bit of lighthearted conversation, and feeling more than a little awkward now.

'We're on a scientific expedition.'

'Searching for creatures?'

'I have a theory,' said Darwin, looking serious. 'I'm afraid it's proved to be rather controversial. We came here looking for proof.'

'What is this theory? In terms a pirate might understand.'

'It is not something to be taken lightly. It will make you look at the world with fresh eyes. Things may never seem the same again,' said Darwin, in a spooky voice.

'Go on,' said the Pirate Captain, his curiosity bitten.

Darwin gave a dramatic pause.

'In short, I believe that a monkey, properly trained, given the correct dietary regime, and dressed in fancy clothes, can be made indistinguishable from a human gentleman. I believe he would cease to be a monkey, and become more a . . . a Man-panzee, if you will.'

A silence held the room. One of the pirates whistled.

'I . . . see. A Man-panzee?' said the Pirate Captain.

'But because of my outlandish theories I have made some powerful enemies—primarily, the Bishop of Oxford,' said Darwin, unable to keep the bitterness out of his voice.

'He finds it offensive?'

'He most certainly does!'

'Because it contravenes his religious beliefs?'

'Oh no! Nothing to do with that, my dear Pirate Captain. The Bishop of Oxford recently became the largest shareholder in P. T. Barnum's world-famous Circus of Freaks.' Darwin leant forward with a conspiratorial air. 'The circus has been making a killing of late, because all of London Town is entranced by its latest exhibit . . . the fantastical Elephant Man. Have you heard of him?'

'Aarrr. He was on show last time we were in England,' said the Pirate Captain. 'A real disappointment as I remember. Doesn't even

have a trunk. The trick is not to treat him like a gentleman, because he always starts crying if you do that.'

'Anyhow, the Bishop of Oxford is clearly alarmed that my Man-panzee might steal his Elephant Man's thunder. So he denounced my ideas as blasphemous—he even said there was a bit in the Bible about how it was a sin to dress a monkey up in a waistcoat, but when asked for the page reference, he claimed to have forgotten.'

Darwin was clearly on the verge of an angry rage.

'So I joined this expedition in an attempt to find a suitable specimen. Only now I have received word from England that my brother Erasmus has gone missing! I believe he has been kidnapped by the Bishop of Oxford as a means of safeguarding against my successful return. I fear the Bishop intends to do him some great harm unless I abandon my research.'

'Does that mean you've had some success?' asked one of the pirates.

'Come, let me show you.'

Darwin and FitzRoy led the pirates to an adjoining cabin. The pirates gasped, for though the room was dark and cramped, they could still make out its sole occupant. Sitting in a leather-backed armchair was a monkey with the best posture any of the pirates had ever seen. Dressed in an expensive-looking silk suit, with a pipe in his mouth, the creature peered at the pirates through a gold-rimmed monocle. He appeared to be sipping on some sort of cocktail—the Pirate Captain thought he could smell gin. The monkey looked as if he had been freshly shaved, but he was still recognisably a monkey, though if you squinted he might have passed for a wizened old man, or a gigantic walnut.

'Obviously he cannot talk,' said Darwin, turning on a few gaslights. 'But he is able to carry on a conversation by use of flash cards. Though I expect that sometime in the future, technology will move on, so that rather than having to rely on the cards he'll

be able to use . . . oh, I don't know, refrigerator magnets, something like that.'

The monkey straightened his cravat, and held up a series of cards in quick succession.

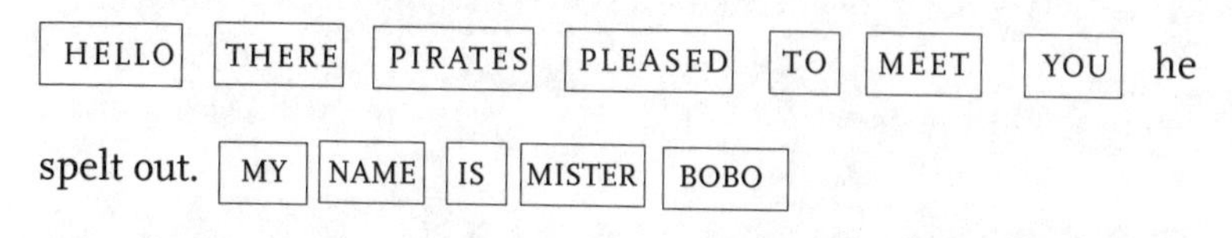

he spelt out.

HELLO THERE PIRATES PLEASED TO MEET YOU
MY NAME IS MISTER BOBO

'Erm, pleased to meet you too,' said the Pirate Captain, who, truth be told, felt like an idiot talking to a monkey, even one as finely dressed as this.* He turned to Darwin, 'It's a fantastic achievement.'

'Yes, Mister Bobo is by far my most promising specimen. I'm glad you didn't hit him with a cannonball. Please, let me give you a demonstration.' Darwin turned to the dapper little creature. 'Mister Bobo, would you tell us how one goes about being a proper gentleman?'

The monkey appeared deep in thought, and then shuffled through his pack of flash cards.

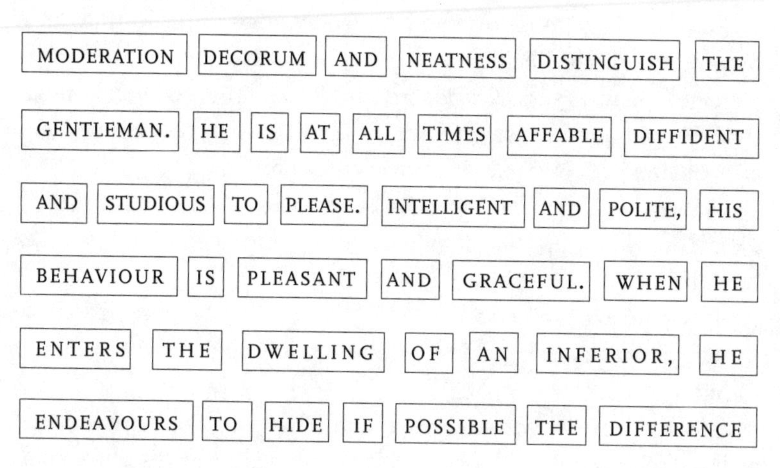

MODERATION DECORUM AND NEATNESS DISTINGUISH THE
GENTLEMAN. HE IS AT ALL TIMES AFFABLE DIFFIDENT
AND STUDIOUS TO PLEASE. INTELLIGENT AND POLITE, HIS
BEHAVIOUR IS PLEASANT AND GRACEFUL. WHEN HE
ENTERS THE DWELLING OF AN INFERIOR, HE
ENDEAVOURS TO HIDE IF POSSIBLE THE DIFFERENCE

*You share about 98.6 per cent of your DNA with a common chimpanzee. And upwards of 99 per cent of your DNA with a pirate!

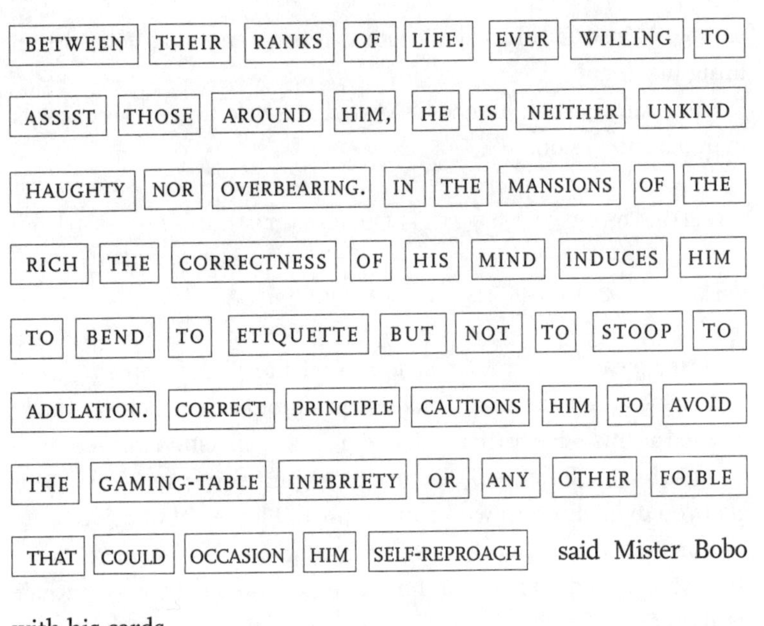

said Mister Bobo with his cards.

BETWEEN THEIR RANKS OF LIFE. EVER WILLING TO
ASSIST THOSE AROUND HIM, HE IS NEITHER UNKIND
HAUGHTY NOR OVERBEARING. IN THE MANSIONS OF THE
RICH THE CORRECTNESS OF HIS MIND INDUCES HIM
TO BEND TO ETIQUETTE BUT NOT TO STOOP TO
ADULATION. CORRECT PRINCIPLE CAUTIONS HIM TO AVOID
THE GAMING-TABLE INEBRIETY OR ANY OTHER FOIBLE
THAT COULD OCCASION HIM SELF-REPROACH

'You see? Not exactly perfect, but he makes a good stab at it. For a monkey,' said Darwin.

Flash cards were hardly the fastest way of communicating, and by now the pirates' bellies were rumbling. Also their pirate boots were getting wet as the *Beagle* started to sink, so they'd been hoping that the young scientist might have finished his speech, but Darwin, obviously proud of his discovery, went on.

'Naturally, I intended to find a better class of tailor back in England, one who might be able to do something to conceal his huge unsightly ass.'

'It *is* a big ass,' agreed a pirate.

'How have you been able to train him so well?' asked the Pirate Captain.

'Mostly fire.' Darwin nodded at some hot tongs hanging on the wall, and Mister Bobo looked a bit frightened. 'But it's all been a waste. I'll never be able to show him off to high society, for fear of some terrible retribution suffered by Erasmus. And even if I did

intend to confront the black-hearted Bishop of Oxford, now I don't even have a means of returning home to England. I am lost.'

And with that Darwin started to bawl like a baby. The pirates stared at the floor, and shifted from foot to foot. They couldn't help but feel a little responsible for the scientist's predicament, on account of their scuppering his boat with all those cannonballs. The pirates had a bit of a discussion amongst themselves. Then the Pirate Captain turned to Darwin.

'I don't much care to be hung in irons.* And that's what we've been promised if we ever set foot in England again. But we don't want to see you and your Man-panzee bested by this scoundrel Bishop you've told us about. So just as soon as we've eaten, us pirates will help you rescue your brother, and get Mister Bobo accepted by Victorian high society and everything.'

Darwin went to plant a big kiss on the Pirate Captain's salty face, but then thought better of it and shook him by the hand. Everybody cheered, even Mister Bobo.

---

*As a warning to seafarers it was common practice in Britain and her overseas colonies to put the bodies of notorious pirates on display near the entrance to a port. Several pirates were hanged at Execution Dock on the banks of the Thames in London.

Five

TRAPPED IN QUICKSAND!

The pirates helped Darwin, FitzRoy, and the crew of the *Beagle* shift their luggage from the slowly sinking boat.

'You'll have to sleep in a hammock, I'm afraid,' said the Pirate Captain. 'They're quite comfortable, but they can leave a criss-cross pattern on your buttocks.'

'Are you sure there's room?' asked Darwin, anxious not to be too much trouble.

'Don't worry about that. We'll make room,' said the Pirate Captain, adding with a merry wink, 'Truth is I've been meaning to have some of my pirates walk the plank for ages, I just haven't got round to it.'*

'Walk the plank? That's barbaric!' blurted out Darwin, before remembering that pirate ways are not necessarily the ways of other men. 'I'm sorry, it's just . . . there's really no need to go to those lengths. We'll sleep standing up, like bats.'

The Pirate Captain swatted his objections away.

*Plank-walking as a punishment was nothing like as common as TV and films would suggest, but there is one report from *The Times* of 23 July 1829 of Dutch sailors being compelled to walk the plank by pirates from Buenos Aires.

'Honestly, it's been far too long since we did this. Lately, if a pirate has been annoying us, we've just shaved off an eyebrow or drawn a little moustache on his face whilst he sleeps, but it's no real substitute.'

He rummaged about in a large pine box that one of the crew had fetched from the hold.

'Oh, I haven't seen those for a while!' said the Captain, pulling out a garish pair of old pirate trousers. 'What was I thinking?! Ah, here it is.'

He blew the dust off a big plank of wood. Seeing that Darwin and FitzRoy were still looking a bit concerned, the Pirate Captain shot them a reassuring grin.

'Listen,' he said. 'It's not like I make any old pirate take the terrible walk. Strictly fools and lubbers. It's for the good of the species.'

As soon as the pirate boat reached shark-infested waters, the Pirate Captain, with a steely glint in his eye, gave the order to drop anchor. There was a carnival atmosphere on board once the pirates realised that there was going to be some plank-walking. Darwin and FitzRoy looked on aghast as the Pirate Captain called out the first name.

The ratty-haired pirate called Marcus was the first to go. He begged and pleaded and cried like a little girl, but a few cutlass prods from some of the other pirates soon had him edging along the narrow piece of wood. He stopped at the end, and began to blubber again, so the pirate with a scarf crept up behind him, and quickly pushed him into the sea. The remaining pirates crowded round the edge of the deck, craning their necks to see ratty-haired Marcus desperately splashing about. For a bit, nothing much happened, but all of a sudden the water around him seemed to churn and crash in on itself, there was a scream, a cracking sound, and then a cloud of red spread out like a flower over the blue sea. The cloud of red wasn't a flower—

it was blood coming out of Marcus. The pirates all gave a mighty cheer.*

The other pirates singled out by the harsh but undeniably fair Pirate Captain were dispatched in similar fashion. They included the balding archaeologist pirate called Stan; the rich pirate who tried to pass himself off as a hippy, whose name the Pirate Captain had forgotten; the pirate who had taught the Pirate Captain geography at Pirate Academy; a boring pirate from Oxford called Adam; and the stupid pirate who had got in the Pirate Captain's way when he was trying to eat pancakes. A late addition was a male model pirate whom the Pirate Captain hadn't even met.

As soon as the plank-walking was finished, the Pirate Captain pointed the boat towards England, and all the remaining pirates and their guests went belowdecks for a feast. For a change the pirates had lamb instead of ham, with the usual accompaniment of green mint sauce and a salad. As a nice added touch the roast lamb was sprinkled with a little minced parsley. A few of Darwin's monkeys had also been served up as an appetiser. There had been some debate as to the best way to cook a monkey, but eventually the pirates had decided to treat the monkeys as if they were turkeys, so after the sinews had been drawn from the legs and thighs, and the monkeys carefully trussed, they were stuffed with sausage meat and veal. It was all served with gravy and bread sauce. Too late the Pirate Captain realised that he had invited Mister Bobo to the feast, but if the creature was put out at being offered a slice of his chimpanzee brethren he was far too polite to say anything.

'So . . . have you been a pirate captain long?' asked Darwin, gulping down a mug of grog.

*Despite the fearsome reputation of sharks, more people are actually killed each year by pigs. Also, sharks have no bones—their skeletons are made entirely from cartilage.

‘Goodness me! Long as I can remember,’ said the Pirate Captain.

‘You’ve never considered as a career something a little more orthodox?’

‘I dare say I’ve considered it, but the fact is I’m a slave to pirating! I love it! The salty sea air, the exotic locations, the shiny gold. Especially the shiny gold.’

‘I can see you’re pretty good at it,’ said Darwin graciously. Pirates seemed a lot more civilised than he had expected. He was unaware of the tremendous effort most of the crew were making in an attempt to eat in a respectable manner because they didn’t want to look sloppy in front of visitors. Several of them were wearing their most jaunty sashes, and they had spent all day cleaning the boat from top to bottom.

‘I have to say,’ said Darwin, looking misty-eyed, ‘a part of me is quite jealous of your villainous lifestyle. Free from the tyranny of what society deems acceptable! Masters of your own fate! Living beyond the law! Us scientific types must seem rather dull to your piratical eyes.’

‘Not at all,’ said the Pirate Captain to his guest. ‘I’ve always been interested in science. Perhaps, as a scientist, you’ll be able to answer a question that has perplexed me for many years.’

‘I’ll certainly do my best.’

‘Tell me—scientifically speaking—who do you think the tallest pirate in the world is?’

‘Erm. It’s a bit outside my field of expertise,’ replied Darwin apologetically.

‘Ah well. Perhaps I’m destined never to know!’ said the Pirate Captain with a wistful air.

‘Darwin’s not the only one with a scientific theory,’ said FitzRoy. ‘I’ve been doing some fascinating work to do with weather prediction. I hope to found a meteorological office when I return to London.’

Nobody at the table was at all interested in what FitzRoy was

talking about, so he trailed off and stared miserably at his soup.*

Darwin chewed on a monkey's paw. 'How long do you expect it will take us to reach England?'

'There's plenty of hams on board, if that's what you're worried about,' replied the Pirate Captain reassuringly. 'But let's see now . . .' The Captain gazed into the middle distance and furrowed his brow to make it look like he was doing some difficult calculations in his head. In fact he was wondering if anybody had noticed how shiny his boots were, because he'd had the pirate with a scarf spend the whole morning polishing them. 'I should say we'd reach England by Tuesday or thereabouts, with a decent wind behind us. It would be a lot quicker than that if we could just sail straight there, but I was looking at the nautical charts, and it's a good job I did, because it turns out there's a dirty great sea serpent right in the middle of the ocean! It has a horrible gaping maw and one of those scaly tails that looks like it could snap a boat clean in two. So I thought it best to sail around that.'

FitzRoy frowned. 'I think they just draw those on maps to add a bit of decoration. It doesn't actually mean there's a sea serpent there.'

The galley went rather quiet. A few of the pirate crew stared intently out of the portholes, embarrassed at their Captain's mistake. But to everyone's relief, instead of running somebody through, the Pirate Captain just narrowed his eyes thoughtfully.

'That explains a lot,' he said. 'I suppose it's also why we've never glimpsed that giant compass in the corner of the Atlantic. I have to say, I'm a little disappointed.'

Darwin thoughtfully picked a piece of macaque from between his teeth. 'You know, this reminds me of the time I was first searching

*In 1865 FitzRoy committed suicide at his home in Upper Norwood. In 1862 he had published *The Weather Book.*

for monkeys, on a nameless isle somewhere off the coast of South America,' he said, a far-off look in his eyes. 'It was close to Christmas, and the others in my expedition had been wanting to get home to their families and loved ones, but I was sure we were near to success, so I insisted that we stay. For several more days my search continued in vain, until I stumbled across a single severed monkey's claw in the heart of the steaming jungle. At last I had proof that there were monkeys to be found in the region, and I took the claw back to show the others. The rest of the expedition said it was disgusting and probably diseased, and they complained that I hadn't found a single complete monkey in six months. Once again they demanded that we should set sail, but I knew that in their heart of hearts they would be as disappointed as myself to return home empty-handed. So I ordered them to stay another month. But that very night strange and terrible things began to happen.'

'What sort of things?' asked the sassy pirate, wide-eyed.

'Strange messages appeared. The words "Darwin is an idiot" were written on my sleeping bag. My toothpaste went missing, and so did my shoes. Then, a few days later, I awoke to find all my fellow scientists gone, vanished as if into thin air, and the food and boat with them. If it hadn't been for a passing freighter, I might have perished on that godforsaken isle. I realised at once that the monkey's claw must carry a terrible curse, so I flung it back into the jungle from whence it came.'

'What had happened to the others in your expedition?'

'The strangest thing of all. When I returned to England I found the rest of the expedition sipping cocktails in our gentlemen's club. They seemed very surprised to see me. It turns out that they could have sworn they had told me they were setting sail, but when they realised I wasn't aboard it was too late, and for some strange reason they had all forgotten the way back to the island. I told them about the curse of the claw and they all agreed that must have been the cause of my misfortune.'

'What happened to the claw?' asked the Pirate Captain fearfully.

'We may never know . . . ,' said Darwin, making a creepy face. The candles flickered eerily, and the shadows seemed to draw in around the room. His frightening story finished, the pirates looked at each other nervously. None of them was keen to get to bed.

'Well, good night.'

'Night.'

'What was that? Can you hear creaking?'

'We're on a boat, there's always creaking.'

'Ha! Yes. Of course. That must be it.'

'What a stupid story that man told.'

'It was stupid, wasn't it?'

Six

PIRATES AHOY!

After a brief encounter with some lovely but black-hearted lady pirates,* the pirate boat finally arrived in the sleepy seaside town of Littlehampton, on the south coast of England. Houses were still cheap there, compared to London prices, but of course there was always the risk of flooding. The beach was pretty good, and there was a lot of that seaweed that looks a bit like brains lying about. A couple of the pirates did impressions of the zombie pirates and said, 'Brains! Feed me brains!' and pretended to stuff the seaweed into their mouths.

'We must make haste to London,' said Darwin, fetching his suitcase up onto the beach, 'to meet my fellow scientists at the Royal Society.'

'Yes, quite right. Not a moment to lose!' agreed the Pirate Captain. 'Except a few of the men noticed an amusement arcade just along from here, and I promised them they could go. It has a gigantic slide and everything.'

'But Erasmus! He could be in all sorts of danger!'

*Lady pirates were rare but not unheard of. A famous example was Anne Bonny, who became the lover of Calico Jack and was tried for piracy in Spanish Town, Jamaica.

The Pirate Captain's eyes flashed red like hot cannonballs.

'I'm sure your brother wouldn't begrudge my crew a little entertainment after such a hard voyage,' he said, a hint of steel in his voice.

'Oh, very well,' replied Darwin, sulkily.

The pirate crew were excited to be visiting an arcade, but it proved to be a dilapidated affair. The only halfway decent machines consisted of an ingenious mechanical series of shelves, which all shunted backwards and forwards, each shelf laden with piles of silvery doubloons. By putting a doubloon into a little slot the hope was to knock several doubloons over the edge of a precipice, where they could be collected. The pirates spent ages on one of the machines, because there was an actual pocket watch resting on the doubloons near the edge, but no matter how much of their treasure they fed into the gas-powered beast, the loot wouldn't fall down—it was almost as if the doubloons were stuck there with glue. A couple of the pirates got into trouble for trying to shake the machine, and they had to run outside and hide behind a man selling ice creams.

'This is rubbish,' said the pirate who was eating some candy floss, and the other pirates agreed, so they walked back down the beach to where Darwin and FitzRoy were waiting. Seeing them, Darwin leapt to his feet and gathered up his luggage once more.

'So, are we ready? There is a locomotive to London that leaves in half an hour,' said Darwin, eager to be off.

'Yes,' said the Pirate Captain. 'We must hurry! Oh look—a nautical-themed crazy golf! Let's have a go!'

'But the train . . . ,' said Darwin, with a touch of resignation.

'Nautical-themed! Do you think that's a genuine ship's anchor? It's very realistic. You and FitzRoy can play as a team if you want,' said the Pirate Captain, handing him a putter.

Darwin could see there was no point arguing with the Pirate Captain once he had made up his mind.

The Pirate Captain swung his golf club, and the ball pinged away, only to hit the side of a big metal anchor and roll back to where it had started.

'That's lucky, it's a free drop,' said the Pirate Captain, picking up his ball and placing it about a foot from the hole. 'Because I hit the anchor.'

'Eh? Are you sure about that?' asked Darwin, instantly wishing he had kept quiet.

'Yes. Because I hit the anchor,' repeated the Pirate Captain, this time in a menacing tone that spoke of rum and murder.

The pirate with a scarf hit his ball, which bounced off a barrel, hit the anchor, and rolled back again. He went to pick it up.

'What do you think you're doing?' roared the Pirate Captain incredulously.

'My free drop. Because I hit the anchor.'

'But you hit the barrel first!'

'Erm . . . yes.'

'So that invalidates any effect the anchor might have.'

'Oh.'

'And by hitting the barrel and then the anchor, you've put the anchor permanently out of play for everybody else. So no more free drops, I'm afraid.'

In all, they played three rounds of crazy golf and the Pirate Captain won all three, but everyone had a good time. As they ambled back along the sea front, the Pirate Captain told them all an exciting story about the time he lost a leg in a fight with a Great White Shark. FitzRoy remarked that the Pirate Captain seemed to have two perfectly good legs, at which point the Pirate Captain went a bit quiet and pretended to be very interested in a shell he had picked up.

'We'd better be off to rescue my brother,' said Darwin.

'Yes,' said the Pirate Captain. 'We shall. Just as soon as we've paid a visit to that sweet factory to find out how they get the words inside sticks of rock. Aargh! I'm just pulling your leg. Don't look so worried. I've sailed the seven seas, and I've never had an unsuccessful adventure yet!'

'Really? You've sailed all seven seas?' asked Darwin admiringly.

'Every last one!'

'What *are* the seven seas? I've always wondered.'

'Aaarrr. Well, let's see . . . ,' said the Pirate Captain, scratching his craggy forehead. 'There's the North Sea. And that other one, the one near Mozambique. And . . . what's that one in Hyde Park?'

'The Serpentine?'

'That's the one. How many's that, then? Three. Um. There's the sea with all the rocks in it . . . I think they call it Sea Number Four. Then that would leave . . . uh . . . Grumpy and Sneezy . . .'

Darwin was starting to look a little less impressed.

'Would you look at that big seagull!' said the Pirate Captain, quickly ducking into a beach hut.

Seven

TARGET: PIRATES!

And so the pirates and their companions arrived in Victorian London. It was not the London you would recognise from nowadays—there was no Millennium Wheel or Tate Modern or Eurostar or Starbucks or Millennium Dome or Jubilee Line Extension or any of the other things you probably assume have always existed. There was soot and orphans everywhere, and gaslit cobbled streets full of fog and sinister gentlemen out for a night of illicit murder. It was a strict and unforgiving society; looking at a piano, eating too much butter, dancing with elan—the sour-faced Queen Victoria forbade all these things. Also, it was always raining in the London of themadays—dirty grey slabs of rain that left everywhere shining and slippery.

To Darwin's continued dismay the Pirate Captain insisted they visit London Zoo before doing anything else. All the pirates agreed that it wasn't as good as Berlin Zoo, which they had visited on a previous adventure to Germany, and that it had far too large a hoofed-animals section. 'Who cares about hoofed animals? They never get

up to anything!' said the pirate in green, wisely. The chimps were an especially sorry bunch—the chimps in Berlin Zoo had put on quite a display when the pirates had visited, shouting and weeing right in front of shocked tourists, but the London chimps just rocked back and forth, obviously suffering from zoo-psychosis. Mister Bobo stared sadly at them through the glass, a bit embarrassed on their behalf. The albino pirate noticed a sign which pointed to an exhibit of 'The Most Destructive Animal in the World!' Some of the pirates had bets on whether it would be a bear or a shark, but it turned out to be a big mirror. The most destructive animal in the world was mankind itself! Especially pirates! But to show they weren't all bad, two of the pirates decided to sponsor a polar bear.*

After that, even though Darwin kept on looking pointedly at his watch and rolling his eyes, the pirates went shopping in the West End. Several of them got themselves the latest pirate stylings from Carnaby Street. Apparently that year's fashion could be summed up as 'the more buckles the better!' and the pirates now made a loud clanking noise as they walked along. They also all bought a few postcards and Union Jacks. The pirate in green who wanted to have the Pirate Captain drawn on his arm had managed to find a tattoo parlour in the Soho district, and now carried a bundle of pamphlets with titles like 'Inky Skin', which he said he'd picked up because he was now very interested in tattoos, and not because of the pictures of ladies wearing next to nothing, but the other pirates weren't sure they believed him.

As they trailed down Charing Cross Road, finally exhausted from their exciting day out in the Big Smoke, the Pirate Captain noticed a poster stuck to a pillar box. It said in olden-days writing:

*London Zoo is still going today, and this year's baby-bear-naming competition was won by Sandokan Soloman for his name, 'Ursula'.

P.T. BARNUM

(in association with the Bishop of Oxford)

is proud to present his

W O R L D - F A M O U S

Circus of Freaks

featuring the Elephant Man! The Mermaid! A Beard of Bees!

Tuesday, Wednesday, Thursday, Friday and Saturday

are

'Ladies' Nights!' Free entry all day to ladies.

'That's a lot of ladies' nights,' said the Pirate Captain thoughtfully.

'Yes,' said Darwin. 'It's a peculiar thing. I heard from my cousin that ever since the Bishop of Oxford became the major shareholder in the circus—about seven or eight months ago—the number of ladies' nights has risen dramatically, to at least five a week.'

'I wonder if that foreshadows anything sinister?' said the Pirate Captain.

'We shouldn't leap to conclusions, just because the unspeakable Bishop is our enemy,' said Darwin reasonably. 'After all, it may be that he feels sorry for ladies, and thinks they could do with some free entertainment.'

'Why would he feel sorry for ladies?' asked the albino pirate.

'Well, what with so many of them going missing lately, and then being found washed up in the River Thames, all shrivelled and lifeless.'

'How long has *that* been going on?'

'Oooh, about seven or eight months, I should say.'

The conversation was interrupted when the pirate with a scarf spotted a policeman coming along the street towards them.

The pirates and their companions quickly ducked into Leicester Square.

'It's not safe on the streets for you pirates,' said Darwin, still pushing Mister Bobo along in a pram so as not to draw any unwanted attention. 'Upstairs in the Natural History Museum there is the Royal Society Gentlemen's Club, where we might plan our course of action.'

'Will they have grog there?' asked the sassy pirate.

'Yes. And cigars. But I don't think they'll let pirates in. And Lord knows what my colleagues would think if they saw me associating with sea dogs like you.'

The pirates were a bit hurt by this, and Darwin was quick to try to save their feelings.

'I mean, obviously, FitzRoy and I know that you're stand-up fellows, it's just the other members . . . they may be rather quick to judge.'

'There's only one thing for it, then,' said the Pirate Captain, a gleam in his eye. 'We'll have to disguise ourselves as scientists!'

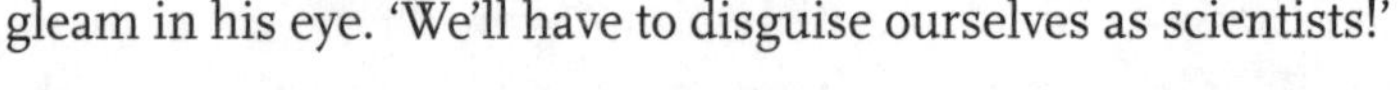

Holding pens and rulers, and with white lab coats covering their piratical paraphernalia, the pirates followed Darwin into the Royal Society Gentlemen's Club.* There were several famous scientists present, some sitting around smoking, some engaged in animated discussion about the latest scientific topic, and some just watching the dancing girls. The smell of opium hung heavily in the air.

'Anyhow,' one of the scientists was saying to another, 'there simply isn't room in the museum's Fishes Hall, so we've decided to pretend to the public that a whale is actually a mammal without any legs. It's patently ridiculous—I mean to say, just look at the

*The Royal Society was set up in 1660, and many famous scientists have been members, including Robert Boyle, Robert Hooke, and John Venn. Why not try drawing a Venn Diagram of 'pirates' (A) and 'ham' (B) and 'barrels of tar' (C)? How large is the intersection (X)?

thing, it's a gigantic fish if ever you saw one—but mum's the word! In my experience the public will believe just about anything, so long as you write it down on a little piece of card.'

The Pirate Captain coughed.

'Goodness! Look, everybody, it's Darwin! Darwin's back!' exclaimed one of the scientists with bushy sideburns, and everybody crowded round Darwin and FitzRoy, slapping them on the shoulders and asking questions. It was a couple of minutes before Darwin could get a word in edgeways.

'Uh, these here are some scientists I met on my travels,' he said, indicating the disguised pirates. 'I hope you'll make them feel welcome.'

'Sorry. We're forgetting our manners. It's just so good to see Charles back, alive and well. One hears such stories about life on the high seas. Giant squids and pirates and the like,' said a genuine scientist, shaking the Pirate Captain's hand. 'What sort of science do you do?'

'What sort of science? Well . . . it's mainly . . . chemicals,' said the Pirate Captain, thinking on his feet. 'There's a lot of stirring things together. And then writing things down, of course.'

'Fascinating,' said the scientist. 'And what about you? What's your field?' he added, turning to the pirate with a hook for his hand.

The pirate with a hook for his hand didn't know what to say, but the quick-witted Pirate Captain cut in deftly. 'My modest colleague does a lot of work with minerals. He likes gold best. He heats it up, with matches.'

'Surely, as a man of science, you'd use a Bunsen burner?'

'Did I say matches? Yes, I meant Bunsen burner. It's been a long day.' The Pirate Captain shrugged apologetically.

The pirates managed to do a pretty decent job of mingling with the scientists, nodding politely and saying 'Really?' a lot as they listened

to them drone on about their latest inventions and discoveries, but the Pirate Captain soon found himself involved in a particularly awkward conversation about molecules, so he was relieved when FitzRoy interrupted him before it got to the stage where he had to say if he was for or against them.

'As a fellow nautical man, there's somebody I'd like you to meet,' said FitzRoy, grabbing the Pirate Captain by the sleeve of his lab coat and dragging him over to shake hands with a fresh-faced young scientist.

'This is James Glaisher, the famous meteorologist,' said FitzRoy. The Pirate Captain wasn't sure what a meteorologist did, but he suspected it was something boring.

'James and I have long held the belief that the weather does not operate in some capricious manner, and that with sufficient information, it should be possible to give advance warning of storms at sea. Our voyage has only served to further convince me.'

The Pirate Captain made sure he was doing his best interested-face whilst he wondered what time scientists tended to eat dinner.

'So tell me, James,' continued FitzRoy, 'how have the experiments been going? Did you get a chance to make the modifications I suggested for your ship?'

'What's this?' said the Pirate Captain, his ears pricking up, eager to find a topic he could make head or tail of. 'You have a ship? Why, I have a boat myself!'

'I'm afraid it's not that kind of a ship,' explained the scientist.* 'For some time now, FitzRoy and I have pursued the idea of a motorised weather balloon. I believe it to be the world's first lighter-than-air-ship. A dirigible, if you will.'

'A lighter-than-air-ship?' said the Pirate Captain, rubbing his hairy chin. 'How many cannons does it have? My boat has twelve cannons.'

*James Glaisher of the Magnetic and Meteorological Department at the Greenwich Observatory made a series of twenty-nine balloon ascents in the nineteenth century to investigate barometric pressure at altitude.

'Cannons? It doesn't have *any* cannons.'

'You're not going to be much cop when it comes to plundering if you haven't got any cannons!' the Pirate Captain snorted imperiously.

'Plundering? I'm not sure you understand. We've not invented the airship to go plundering.'

'So what on earth *is* it for?' asked the Pirate Captain.

'For? What is all science "for"!' exclaimed the scientist. 'Pushing back frontiers! The thrill of discovery! Advancing the sum total of human knowledge and endeavour! And looking down ladies' tops.'

Over dinner Darwin told the story of his voyage, missing out the bit with the pirates, then he showed off Mister Bobo, who performed impeccably and proved excellent when it came to the after-dinner charades, making everybody laugh as he acted out Daniel Defoe's *Journal of the Plague Year.* All of the scientists agreed that Mister Bobo was a breakthrough, but none of them knew what was to be done about the predicament of Erasmus. A glum gloom settled over the table, and even Darwin's pet bulldog, Huxley, whimpered as it ate the scraps of ham surreptitiously fed to it under the table by the pirate with a scarf.

It was time for action. The Pirate Captain slammed down his After Eight mint with a mighty crash.

'It's clear to me what must be done,' he told the assembled scientists and pirates-dressed-as-scientists. 'Darwin must go ahead and announce a lecture tour with Mister Bobo as if nothing were wrong. I'll get my crew—my scientist crew, that is—to put up posters, and we'll hold the first lecture in this very museum, tomorrow night.'

'But what about the repercussions? Until I know Erasmus is safe, how can I dare?' said Darwin, aghast.

'If my years of experience solving crimes has taught me anything,' said the Pirate Captain, looking reassuringly nonchalant by tipping his chair back dangerously, 'it's that you can't catch a mouse without cheese!'

'Your years of experience solving crimes? But you're a pirate,' whispered Darwin. 'Surely that doesn't involve much detective work?'

'Aarrr,' roared the Pirate Captain, because it seemed a good way to end the conversation.

Eight

BATTLING THE OCTOPUS!

The next morning, waking up for the first time in three years in a proper bed with fresh linen that didn't stink of fish and monkeys, Darwin felt a great deal better about things. Before he had retired for the night the Pirate Captain had taken him aside and gone on to explain his piratical plan. He reasoned that they had no means of ascertaining the whereabouts of Erasmus until the evil Bishop of Oxford showed his face. By announcing the lecture tour with Mister Bobo they would force the Bishop's hand, and he would be sure to turn up in order to try threatening Darwin into backing down. The Bishop would be expecting scientists. What the Bishop wouldn't be expecting were pirates! At this point the plan got a bit hazy, but Darwin felt confident in the Pirate Captain's abilities nonetheless. He propped himself up on his pillows and flicked through that morning's edition of *The Times*, pretending not to look at the more salacious pictures of table legs. There was another big headline about a mysteriously shrivelled lady being found bobbing about in the Thames, and an article in the Style section where he saw that for the fifth year running, 'sinister and macabre' was still very much in vogue when it came to the

Victorian gentleman's interior design choices. He sighed. With sunlight streaming in through the window, and a plate of toast already brought to him by the Royal Society's butler, Darwin was tempted to spend the whole morning in bed, but he had a lot to sort out, so he shook Mister Bobo awake and started preparing for the evening's lecture. A lecture, he pondered, that could make his name as a scientist—and, by that token, hopefully lead to a good deal more success with women.

In one of the Royal Society's bathrooms just down the hall the Pirate Captain was busy flossing.

'Are you going to be in there much longer?' asked an unfamiliar voice with an impatient knock. The Pirate Captain flung open the door, ready to run through with his shiny cutlass whosoever it happened to be, but then he remembered he was supposed to be a mild-mannered scientist, not a bloodthirsty Terror of the High Seas. So instead he fixed the knave who had the cheek to interrupt his toiletries with a steely stare. He recognised one of the scientists from dinner.

'Yes,' growled the Pirate Captain. 'I am going to be in here much longer. Beards like this don't look after themselves, you know.'

'Right, sorry,' said the scientist, backing away meekly. 'Gosh. You've got a lot of scars.'

The Pirate Captain was wearing only a risqué towel, and he did indeed have a number of scars from previous adventures.

'That's from bumping against scientific apparatus in my laboratory,' explained the Pirate Captain, a murderous gleam in his eyes.

'And is that . . . a treasure map tattooed on your belly?'

'No. It's the periodic table.'

'It doesn't look like the periodic table. X isn't an element.'

The Pirate Captain decided to run the scientist through with his cutlass after all. He washed it off in the sink, attended to his beard,

and then went back to the room he was sharing with some of the other pirates.

'They may know how to make a mechanical pig,' said the Pirate Captain, 'but these scientists have got a lot to learn about manners.'

The other pirates all nodded at this and sucked thoughtfully on their daily ration of limes, except for the pirate with an accordion, who was sucking on a green Starburst because he didn't much care for proper fruit.

'Now, does everybody know what they're doing today? You two'—the Pirate Captain pointed to the albino pirate and the pirate with a hook where his hand should have been—'will help Mr Darwin with anything he needs for his lecture. And you two'—this time he indicated the scarf-wearing pirate and the pirate with an accordion—'will check out P. T. Barnum's Circus. Why is a Bishop involved in running a circus, that's what I want to know. I'm not sure how it fits in with his diabolical plans, but I have my suspicions about the place. It's ladies' night, so you'll have to disguise yourselves as women.'

'It's going to be quite difficult fitting a lady disguise on top of our scientist disguises, which we're already wearing on top of our pirate outfits,' said the scarf-wearing pirate.

'You'll just have to do your best,' said the Pirate Captain. 'I'd go myself, but obviously my luxuriant beard would make it difficult for me to pass as a lady. And don't forget that ladies speak in squeaky voices. Like this—"Hello, I'm a lady!" '

Everybody laughed at the Pirate Captain's brilliant impression of what a lady sounded like.*

'The rest of you pirates go round town and paste up these posters advertising tonight's lecture.'

*Men's vocal cords tend to be thicker than women's, so they produce a deeper tone in exactly the same way that a thick rubber band makes a deeper sound than a thin one when you twang it. You might need to stretch the rubber bands over a biscuit tin to get the full effect.

The Pirate Captain handed out a stack of A4 posters. They were illustrated with a picture of Darwin and Mister Bobo playing chess. Mister Bobo was in Rodin's *The Thinker* pose, and Darwin had thrown his hands up in defeat. The Pirate Captain had drawn the picture himself, and was proud of his effort. Before he became a pirate he was going to be an architect, and he had used his knowledge of perspective and foreshortening to make Mister Bobo's massive monkey behind seem a lot smaller than it was in real life. And he'd managed to give Darwin a genuine look of exasperation at having been bested by a chimp. The only thing about the picture that slightly disappointed the Pirate Captain was Darwin's hands, which looked more like lumpy starfish—for some reason the Pirate Captain had never got very good at drawing hands. Above the picture were the words:

One night only—Mister Charles Darwin will be showing off his fantastic hirsute new friend Mister Bobo—the world's first Man-panzee! Royal Society Lecture Rooms, admission free.

In very small print it was noted that Mister Bobo did not actually play chess to a particularly high standard.

'These are very good, Captain,' said the scarf-wearing pirate, already applying a cherry-coloured lipstick. The Pirate Captain waved away the praise, and mumbled something about how he didn't think it was that good a picture, even though it was obvious how proud he was.

'Now, I hope I can trust you pirates with this. I'm afraid I've got a prior engagement, so I won't be around to help out,' said the Pirate Captain, giving his sternest look to his men, which involved lowering his eyebrows and pursing his lips together.

'What's that, Captain?' asked the accordion-playing pirate, having some difficulty with his bra strap.

'I received a letter this morning, inviting me to attend a Pirate Convention at Earls Court. I'm one of the guests of honour.'

The other pirates occasionally wondered how it was that these letters found their way to their itinerant captain, but somehow they always did.

'A Pirate Convention? You're certain this isn't another of those Royal Navy schemes to trap a whole bunch of pirates?' said the scarf-wearing pirate, his brow furrowed with concern.

'Remember that time they said there was going to be a pirate beauty contest on Mozambique, and we had to shoot our way out?'

'Remember it? Of course I remember it! I still say I was robbed,' pouted the Pirate Captain. His crew nodded—certainly none of them had ever seen another pirate as attractive as their chiselled Captain.

'But, anyhow, the letter came with our secret pirate symbol marked on the envelope. See?' The Pirate Captain pointed to the Jolly Roger* stamped on the seal. 'So it must be the real deal. I'm quite looking forward to it. With any luck I'll be able to sign a few autographs for the kids, and pick up some pirate equipment at bargain prices.'

'All due respects, Captain,' said the pirate in green, feasting on a bowl of cereal, 'but have you really got time to be going off to a Pirate Convention? We're sort of bang in the middle of an adventure here.'

'It's a fair point,' replied the Pirate Captain. 'But I have my reasons. For a start, what with Black Bellamy pulling a fast one on us, the boat's finances aren't looking too healthy, and this could be a chance to make a doubloon or two. Good deeds won't keep us in ham, you know. Secondly, a few of my pirate contacts might come in useful in figuring out just what this Bishop is really up to. And thirdly, I'm the Pirate Captain and I can do whatever the hell I please!'

'Are you planning on wearing that hat to the convention?' asked the pirate in red. The Pirate Captain thought he could detect a certain amount of disapproval in his tone.

---

*Though the name 'Jolly Roger' would lead you to expect a picture of a happy-looking man, it is actually a scary skull above two crossed bones.

'Yes, I am. It happens to be my favourite hat. You may notice that the blue of the trim brings out the blue of my eyes.' The Pirate Captain pointed to the blue trim and then at his blue eyes to emphasise the point.

'Ah. Well, then. I'm sure you know best, Captain.'

'Are you trying to say there's something wrong with my hat?'

'Not at all, Captain. It might not be the most up-to-date choice, but I'm sure there's nothing wrong with that,' said the pirate in red, sounding very much like he thought there was a great deal wrong with it.

'This is a perfectly good pirate hat. It's a tricorn.'

'Exactly.'

'Your point being?'

'It's just . . . nowadays . . . a more Napoleonic design seems to be the choice of the successful pirate. It's generally held to have a touch more . . . *je ne sais quoi*. I'm only saying, is all.'

'My hat has plenty of *je ne sais quoi*. Not to say *joie de vivre*.'

'If you say so.'

'Fine. Hands up, who likes my hat?'

Most of the pirate crew loyally stuck their hands in the air. The pirate in red just shrugged and pretended to be reading a book. Satisfied that the mutinous swab had been put in his place, the Pirate Captain helped himself to another bowl of Cocoa Puffs.

Nine

ENTER THE PIRATE KING!

By twelve o'clock the scarf-wearing pirate and the pirate with an accordion were already sweltering under their multiple disguises. You could hardly hear the clanking of their pirate buckles beneath the layers of lab coat and lady's dress each man wore. They didn't know exactly what it was they were meant to be looking for at the sinister circus—the Pirate Captain had simply told them to keep an eye out for anything suspicious. Looking through the glossy circus brochure the pirate with a scarf thought that it all sounded pretty suspicious—a man with no face, a lady with a phobia for tin foil, an out-of-control teen . . . he was worried that they wouldn't know where to start. The queue to get in stretched all the way down the Mall.

'That's a fetching eye patch. Is it just for show?'

It took the pirate with a scarf a few seconds to realise that the question was being directed at him, and by the young lady just ahead of them in the queue. Looking up, he was so taken aback by how pretty she was he almost forgot to answer in a high-pitched voice instead of his normal pirate voice.

'It's . . . that is . . . I've got an astigmatism,' he stuttered. 'The optician says I have to wear the patch until it goes away.'

'You poor thing,' said the girl, with a look of real concern. 'Would you like a sandwich? It's Serrano ham.'

The pirate with a scarf gratefully took the proffered sandwich. He thought he had better make introductions. 'Thank you. I'm . . . Francine. And this is, erm, Daphne,' he said.

'Jennifer. That's a very shiny accordion you have there, Daphne.'

The pirate with an accordion just grunted, because his lady voice wasn't particularly realistic.

'You're extremely rugged. For a girl,' said Jennifer, turning back to the pirate with a scarf.

'Thank you,' said the pirate, unconsciously flexing the muscles in his back, and knitting his eyebrows together in what he hoped was a suave manner.

'Are you here to see the Mermaid?' asked Jennifer. 'I've heard it's a bit disappointing. Just the top half of a monkey stitched to the bottom half of a fish.'

'Erm, no. That is, not in particular.'

'The albino then?'

'Actually, one of our friends is an albino,' said the pirate brightly.

'Ooh! Is it true that if you ever look directly into their eyes, you turn into an albino yourself? And that they can only eat white things, like vanilla ice cream and milky bars?'

'I don't think so. I'm not entirely sure.'

'I wonder if they can eat mallow?'

Jennifer seemed to be lost in her deliberations about albinos. If the pirate with a scarf had been more poetically minded he'd have thought that her eyes were like a thousand emeralds, glittering in a far-off pirate treasure chest. But he wasn't, so he just thought that she had really *really* green eyes, a bit like seaweed.

'What about you? What are you here to see?' asked the pirate quickly, anxious to keep the conversation going. 'The Elephant Man?'

'Not really. Between you and me'—at this point Jennifer put her mouth alarmingly close to the pirate with a scarf's ear—'I think something sinister is going on at the circus. My sister Beatrice visited it last week, and that's the last we ever saw of her.'

'I think you could be right,' said the pirate, completely forgetting the undercover nature of their mission because of the shape of her neck. 'In fact, we're here to investigate. I'm not even really a lady.'

The pirate with a scarf briefly raised his dress.

'You're a scientist!'

The pirate remembered to lift up his lab coat as well.

'You're a pirate!'

'Yes, but don't tell anybody.'

Half an hour later Jennifer and the two pirates were through the turnstiles and inside the circus itself. The pirate with an accordion pretty quickly started to feel more like the pirate who was a gooseberry, so he wandered off to look at an exhibit that claimed to be 'the dog that wore sunglasses', and left Jennifer and the scarf-wearing pirate to their own devices. The circus was sprawled across St James's Park, and a blanket of thick London fog hung between the various tents. The pair decided to start their investigations with the Elephant Man. He was sitting in the centre of a little hut looking a bit forlorn, whilst a man with a tuba played a few bars of 'Nellie the Elephant' over and over again.

'He doesn't look big enough to have eaten my sister,' said Jennifer. 'But he might know something.'

'We should try to gain his confidence by carrying on a pleasant conversation,' whispered the pirate.

'I'll have a go,' nodded Jennifer. She took a few steps towards the creature and cleared her throat.

'Wow!' she said. 'So you're the Elephant Man! That's some face!'

It wasn't exactly the opening gambit the pirate with a scarf had in mind, but he bit his lip because the closest he had come recently to

having any success with a girl was the time a few weeks before when he had drunk too much rum, and ended up thinking he was in love with the pirate boat's figurehead. The boat's figurehead was certainly attractive, and extremely well carved, but it left him with nasty splinters whenever he tried to give it a hug.

'I'd—uh—prefer it if you called me John,' said the Elephant Man, trying to crack a smile. 'My name is John Merrick.'

'Okay, John it is. So let me get this straight . . . you got turned into an elephant-*man* by being bitten by an actual elephant, is that right? Was the elephant radioactive in any way?' asked Jennifer.

'Ah . . . no. I suffer from a rare genetic condition. It causes the rapid growth of bony tumours. There are no elephants involved. Several unfortunate children are born with it every year.'

'Children are born with it? Is that because their mothers have been bitten by an elephant whilst pregnant? Are you saying that if I got pregnant, I shouldn't visit a zoo?'

'No. Really, the condition has nothing to do with elephants.'

'Would the baby only be affected if the mother was bitten in the belly by an elephant? Or would a bite to the leg do it too?'

'I don't think you're really listening . . . ,' said the Elephant Man with as much patience as he could muster.

'I can tell you're from India, because of the shape of your ears,' added Jennifer triumphantly. The Elephant Man just sighed and shook his head.

'Tell me, John,' Jennifer went on, swiftly changing tack. 'Do you know why this circus has so many ladies' nights? I mean, they're virtually every night! It's suspicious!'

'No. No, I don't. I . . . I don't even know what you're talking about,' said the Elephant Man quickly. The pirate with a scarf thought he saw a flash of fear in the wretch's eyes, but it was hard to tell because his face was such a funny shape.

'Listen. Why don't I sing you a song?' said the Elephant Man, obviously desperate to try to change the subject. He even got up and did a little ungainly jig as he sang.

I look like some ex-pe-ri-ment!
But please believe me I'm a proper gent!
I seem like a monster, but whatcha don't know is,
*I got a scorching case of neurofibromatosis!**

Jennifer and the pirate with a scarf gave up on getting a straight answer, and went to search for any clues that might be evident at the other exhibits. But they had no more luck with the Man Who Could Eat a Bicycle, or the Lady Who Had Had Hiccups for Forty Years, or even with the Girl from Chesterfield Who Would Repeatedly Go Out with Idiots When She Could Do a Great Deal Better for Herself. The pea-soup fog was starting to make their eyes sting, so Jennifer and the pirate ducked inside a tent that was simply marked 'A Special Exhibit for the Ladies'. It didn't seem very special—it was just an empty and badly lit tent as far as the pirate with a scarf could make out.

'It's very dark in here. I can't even see what we're meant to be looking at,' said Jennifer, slipping her hand through her companion's arm. The pirate with a scarf's heart skipped a beat. He couldn't believe how well it was going. Usually by this point with a girl he'd have said something idiotic, or spilt drink all down his front, or chewed with his mouth open, but he'd managed not to do any of those things so far, and he even seemed to be impressing her with some of his nautical anecdotes.

'It must mean a good deal of responsibility, being the first mate on a pirate boat,' said Jennifer, shivering at a sudden breeze that seemed to blow through the tent.

*Or possibly Proteus Syndrome. There is still some debate in medical circles. Contrary to popular belief, Michael Jackson never did purchase the Elephant Man's skeleton from the Royal Hospital. This is a good example of how you shouldn't believe everything that people tell you.

'It's not easy. But I try to look after my crew,' said the pirate. 'I saved a man's life the other day. He got attacked by a huge jellyfish, and I neutralised the sting by pouring a bucket of wee all over him.'

He instantly wished he had instead told her about the time he fought a monstrous manatee, because it cast him in a slightly more heroic light, and didn't involve big buckets of wee. Jennifer had gone very quiet, and looking up from his shoes—he was terrible at making eye contact with girls he liked—the pirate with a scarf was surprised to see her slumping unconscious to the floor. For one frightened moment he thought his conversation might have sent her into a daze, so he was pretty relieved when he felt a chloroform-soaked rag press against his mouth, and blacked out himself.

The pirate with a scarf opened his eyes groggily. His vision seemed to go cloudy, but then he realised it was just his breath condensing on the inside of the massive glass tube in which he now found himself trapped. The tube was attached to some kind of improbable contraption, fashioned of wood and brass and covered in cogs, pipes, and hissing gaskets. Looking to his left, he saw that Jennifer was held in an identical predicament. With a sinking feeling, he realised that yet again a date with a pretty girl had gone horribly wrong. He could just make out that they were in some kind of big square room, with what looked like gigantic stained-glass windows for walls. He gave a peevish sigh—he certainly wasn't enjoying this adventure as much as, say, the Pirates' Adventure on the Island of Rum and Amazons.

'So, young scarf-wearing lady! You and your pretty friend are awake!'

The room was so dingy, and so cluttered with menacing-looking bric-a-brac, that the pirate hadn't noticed a figure dressed all in

black robes* busying about in the corner. It was the iniquitous Bishop of Oxford himself! The pirate with a scarf could tell it was the Bishop because he was wearing a bishop's hat, just like the chess pieces that he had seen the Pirate Captain play with on occasion. The pirate with a scarf preferred Ludo or Snakes and Ladders himself.

'What's all this about, you beast?' asked Jennifer from inside her big glass tube. The Bishop fixed her with a beady stare.

'How old would you take me for?' he asked, as if by way of explanation. Jennifer had never been particularly good at estimating this sort of thing, but she hazarded a guess anyhow.

'Mid-to-late forties?'

'Hah! I'm actually fifty-one years old.'

The Bishop gazed at the pair of them expectantly. Jennifer and the pirate with a scarf just looked blankly back at him. He seemed a bit annoyed that he had to explain things further.

'I keep myself so fresh looking by using this devilish machine to distil the very life-essence from young ladies such as you!' he added impatiently.

'So *you're* responsible for all these grisly murders! I had my bets on it being a member of the Royal Family. Or maybe gypsies,' said Jennifer, wide-eyed and fuming. 'You villain!'

'I must say, Bishop,' said the pirate with a scarf—remembering to keep up his lady voice—'the sack and the drugs. It's not the sort of behaviour I'd expect from a man of the cloth.'

The diabolical Bishop looked almost sheepish.

'I realise that my methods leave a lot to be desired,' he replied with a rather forlorn sigh, 'but you have to appreciate the climate I'm working in. Anyone will tell you how difficult it is to meet a nice girl in a big city like this. So you can understand that in my

*Black looks best on persons who have black in their features (hair, eyes, brows, and lashes), although black can be worn by most people for very dramatic occasions.

case, where I need to meet about a dozen nice girls a week in order to synthesise my ghastly concoction . . . well, it's virtually impossible.'

'I can see why you're not a girl's first choice,' said Jennifer with a sneer. 'If a lady is looking for anything to be planted on her mouth at the end of an evening, it's a kiss, not a dirty old cloth soaked in chloroform. The least I'd expect of a fellow who intends to drain the youthful life-force out of me would be flowers and conversation.'

'Yes, it's a bit much. Do you really need the sinister circus and the swirling fog and the kidnapping? Have you tried a nice coffee shop? I hear that they're great places to pick up us women,' said the pirate helpfully.

'Of course I have!' replied the Bishop with an air of despair. 'But it just never works out. I meet a girl, I laugh a booming maniacal laugh at their anecdotes, just like I've read you're meant to, and I make sure to pay them a compliment—"You've got a lovely hairline, I won't need to shave your temples when I attach you to my nightmarish device"—something like that. But more often than not it's a swift peck on the cheek, thanks for a lovely evening, and I'm home alone in my macabre lair. I just don't have time for it! I'm not getting any younger, you know. Well, I suppose in a manner of speaking I am, but you see my point.'

'I doubt that funny little moustache is doing you any favours,' said Jennifer with an arched eyebrow.

'It's an evil moustache, not a gay moustache,' replied the Bishop with a pout.

'That's why you're so bothered by Darwin's Man-panzee!' exclaimed the pirate. 'You're worried that if Mister Bobo is a roaring success, then all the crowds will forget about the Elephant Man, and they'll flock to see him instead! Without a constant supply of young ladies visiting the circus for you to kidnap, you wouldn't be able to fashion your evil elixir!'

'It's not really an elixir. It's more a sort of facial scrub,'* said the Bishop. 'But listen, I'm not about to let you gab your way out of this. On with the show!'

The Bishop threw an enormous lever, and his horrific machine roared into life. Sparks bounced off the walls, pistons smashed up and down, lights flashed, and bells rang. But just as the contraption seemed to be building to a crescendo there was a sickening metallic gurgle, a belch of acrid black smoke, and everything fell silent.

'Oh, for pity's sake!' moaned the Bishop, giving an apologetic look to his captives. 'Honestly, this has never happened before.' He spent the next few minutes trying fruitlessly to find a fault with the various gears and pulleys and bits of wire that made up his machine. The pirate with a scarf took this opportunity to attempt a bit of romantic small talk with Jennifer, but she seemed a little preoccupied and he could sense that the moment might have passed.

'There's no reason why this shouldn't be working. It's brand new,' said the Bishop tetchily. 'Unless . . . one of you isn't really a lady!'

The pirate with a scarf gulped, and tried to do his most winning lady smile, but then he realised that this just showed off more of his gold teeth.

'There's only one way to find out,' said the Bishop, a nasty reptilian grin playing across his face as he advanced upon Jennifer and the disguised pirate.

Forty minutes later, the two of them reluctantly handed the Bishop their completed psychometric test papers. He pored over the results, and then pointed an accusing finger at the pirate. The scarf-wearing

*The Bishop of Oxford was widely known as 'Soapy' Sam Wilberforce. However, if you look this up on Google, chances are it will ascribe the nickname to his 'slippery ecclesiastical debating skills' rather than his habit of turning ladies into bars of soap.

pirate hung his head in dismay—his skill at spatial awareness and numerical pattern identification compared with his comparative weakness at colour differentiation and verbal reasoning had given away his secret.

'You're no lady!' said the Bishop with a scowl. 'In fact, these test results suggest you're a pirate! Goodness knows what you've done to my machine. It's only designed to work with ladies aged nineteen to twenty-six. You've probably invalidated my warranty, you lousy bum.'

The Bishop unhooked the pirate from his infernal apparatus, and rolled him in his tube over to what looked for all the world like a massive metal cog. Then he opened up the top of the tube, slid the bound pirate out, and fastened him to one of the notches between the cog's gigantic teeth. The Bishop looked at his watch irritably. 'I've got an appointment with a man and his monkey,' he said, turning his attention to Jennifer. 'But I expect you to be a lifeless husk by the time I get back, young lady. No funny business.'

With that, he pulled the big lever again, and went off whistling a show tune. The pirate with a scarf looked on in horror as the life started to drain from what was the first girl in ages who looked as though she might actually have put out for him.

Ten

A DEAD MAN'S CHEST!

Halfway across town the Pirate Captain strode along with big piratical strides. He didn't stare down at his feet and scuttle through the sudden downpour like the sorry rubbernecks who shared the narrow streets with him; he held his head high and seemed almost to be snarling at the sky, willing it to do its worst—he was the Pirate Captain, and he wasn't bothered by a bit of rain.

Just a few minutes later—he walked at quite a pace, and had been known to swing his cutlass at ditherers who blocked his way—the Pirate Captain arrived at the Hotel Metropolitan, where, according to his letter, the Pirate Convention was being held. The concierge, a slight and sweaty man, greeted him in the swanky lobby.

'You must be here for the Pork Convention,' he said with an exaggerated wink.

'Pork Convention? Are you mad? I'm here for the Pirate Convention!' said the Pirate Captain, dumbfounded.

'Ha-ha! A Pirate Convention!' laughed the concierge, nervously brushing some of his few remaining hairs across a shiny scalp. 'Imagine! If you were an otherwise respectable hotel, and you were to hold

a Pirate Convention, why'—the concierge gave a meaningful pause—'you'd probably pretend it was a Pork Convention, or something like that.'

'What's this blathering about pork?'

'I think that's what you're looking for.'

'I'm looking for no such thing! And stop winking at me! I've run men through for less!'

'I was simply saying the word "pork" instead of "pirate" so as not to draw any unwanted attention to the proceedings. It's a kind of clever code. It doesn't really matter anymore,' whispered the concierge, a touch irritably.

'Ah! Yes. I'm here for the Pork Convention,' said the Pirate Captain in a loud voice, adding quietly with a wink of his own, 'I see what you're doing now.'

'If you'll just follow me.'

'Certainly. Is there anywhere I can leave my gammon?'

'I'm sorry?'

'My gammon. It's clever code for "cutlass". I just made it up.'

The concierge led the Pirate Captain through the lobby, which had been smartly decked out with big misleading papier-mâché models of different kinds of pork products—including chops and sausages—across an expensive-looking carpet, and into the hotel's main conference hall. It was full to the brim with pirates from all over the globe. Several of them were roaring, so it was quite noisy, and there was a distinct smell of seaweed about the place. Scanning the room, which read like a *Who's Who* of the nautical underworld, the Pirate Captain recognised a familiar figure. He threaded his way through the crowd.

'Raagh! You lubber!' roared the Pirate Captain.

'What's that? Lubber! Who's calling me a lubber! You cur!' said the pirate, spinning round angrily. He must have been a good seven feet tall, with hands the size of the hams the Pirate Captain usually ate for dinner. Several of the other pirates in the immediate vicinity fell silent, their hands on their cutlasses, expecting trouble. But the

giant pirate held up his arms and proceeded to squeeze the Pirate Captain in an embrace that would have crushed the breath out of lesser men with a more limited lung capacity.

'Why! It's my old friend the Pirate Captain!' bellowed the pirate.

'Scurvy Jake!' said the Pirate Captain, evidently glad to see his former comrade. 'I haven't seen you since that incident on Madagascar!'

'Aaarrr! I was sure they were girls!' said Scurvy Jake with an apologetic shrug.

'What are you doing here, you salty old dog?' laughed the Pirate Captain, giving his friend an affectionate slap on his oversized biceps.

'I'm in the nostalgia business!' said Scurvy Jake, indicating the convention buzzing on around them. 'I mean, after I hung up my eye patch I tried my hand at a few things, but what with the Industrial Revolution, it's all factory work. I'm not cut out for all that fiddly business, haven't got the fingers for it.' Scurvy Jake indicated his fingers, which were the size of bananas.* 'But then I found out how lucrative going on the Pirate Convention circuit can be. You sign a few books, tell a couple of stories, there's plenty of grog in return, and you get free board and lodging to boot. I'm actually a lot better at reminiscing about pirating than I ever was at doing it in the first place.'

Scurvy Jake helped the Pirate Captain to a complimentary glass of rum.†

'Let me show you the ropes,' the giant continued. 'There's a panel quiz later on where fans can ask us a few questions, and everybody tends to hit the bar after that. But right now I'm going to sign a few photos of myself. I charge a doubloon a time. Care to join me?'

As it happened the Pirate Captain had stopped off at a Victorian Snappy Snaps, and was clutching a stack of black-and-white six-by-

*Edible bananas may disappear within a decade if urgent action is not taken to develop new varieties resistant to blight, according to recent studies published in *New Scientist*.

†Rum is the oldest distilled spirit in the world. After he was killed at the Battle of Trafalgar, Lord Nelson's body was preserved in a barrel of his favourite rum. To make a good Mai Tai, you need 1 oz. Dark Rum, 1 oz. Light Rum, 1 oz. Triple Sec, 1/2 oz. Lime Juice, 1/2 oz. Grenadine, 1/2 oz. Orgeat Syrup. Garnish with a pineapple wedge and cherry. Serve in a High Ball.

eights, in which he was doing a very debonair face indeed. He settled down at a table next to Scurvy Jake and pretty soon had a queue of asthmatic-looking kids and creepy middle-aged men lining up in front of him. He'd been sort of hoping that groupies might prove to be a problem—girls who wanted nothing more than to annoy their respectable families by throwing themselves at a handsome Pirate Captain—but it was immediately obvious that they were going to be in short supply.

'Could you sign it to Paul,' said the first fan to come shambling up. 'And maybe put something like "Arrgh! Here be treasure!" I was going to stick it on top of my money box, you see.'

'Certainly. That's very clever.'

'My money box is shaped like a pirate boat.'

'Even better,' said the Pirate Captain, handing him his picture with a grin.

'You're fantastic!' said another eager young boy.

'Ah, I don't know if I'd go that far . . .'

'No, really, you are. I was even going to buy a resin model of you swinging on some rigging, but I only had six shillings, so I got Black Bellamy instead. Have you ever met Black Bellamy? He's my favourite pirate ever!'

'Is that a fact?'

'Oh yes. He's terrific. You're almost as good, though. But why are you wearing a hat like that?'

'This happens to be a very stylish pirate hat.'

'Black Bellamy has some brilliant hats. You should talk to him to find out where he gets his hats from.'

'How would you like to be run through by a genuine pirate cutlass?'

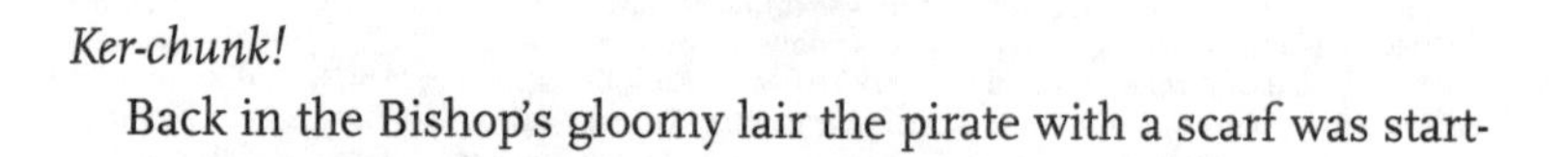

Ker-chunk!

Back in the Bishop's gloomy lair the pirate with a scarf was starting to realise the nature of his predicament. Every few minutes the

massive cog to which he was tied clicked on a few inches. It meshed with another gigantic cog, and he estimated that in a couple of hours he would reach this second set of metallic teeth and be crushed to a pulp of bone and gristle and bits of scarf. The only consolation was that he had found Erasmus Darwin, who was tied between two teeth a little further round, and would be crushed to death several minutes before him. And as the Bishop's monstrous contraption continued to chug away, Jennifer would probably be worse off even sooner. Neither fact was actually much consolation at all.

'Are you okay?' said the pirate to Jennifer.

'My fingertips have started to shrivel up a bit. It's like I've been in the bath too long.'*

'Listen. Assuming we get out of this, how would you like to come out to dinner with me?' The pirate gave what he imagined to be a sexy wink.

'Oh. Well . . . I've sort of got plans,' said Jennifer. Erasmus made a sound like a plane crashing. The pirate with a scarf shot him a bit of a look, and started to wonder why he had bothered getting out of his hammock that morning.

Just then there came the wheezy sound of an accordion. It was an odd little tune that, had he been alive exactly one hundred and fifty years later, the scarf-wearing pirate would have recognised as the first few bars from 'Theme to *Murder, She Wrote*'. Out from behind a gigantic bell stepped the pirate with an accordion. The others were unanimously glad to see him.

'Rescue!' cried Erasmus.

'Daphne!' said Jennifer.

'What took you so long?' asked the pirate with a scarf, in a bit of a strop.

*There's no need to be frightened when your fingers shrivel up after being in the bath. Normally your skin is lubricated with a thin layer of sebum—an oil which acts to waterproof the surface of your body. With prolonged exposure to water the sebum is washed away, which allows water to penetrate into the epidermis by osmosis. The skin becomes waterlogged, resulting in a wrinkled appearance—rather like a monster or an old woman.

'You two wandered off, so I went to the hall of mirrors,' said the pirate with an accordion defensively. 'It was fantastic! One of the mirrors made me look like a little dwarf, but with a big long head! I laughed for ages! And then I got bored of that, so I played a bit of "What shall we do with the drunken sailor?" on my accordion, which happens to be my favourite shanty. Then I tried to find you and your girlfriend.'

'She's not my girlfriend,' said the scarf-wearing pirate with a scowl.

'Bad luck. Anyhow, I noticed the pair of you going into that Special Exhibit for the Ladies, and when you didn't come out for ages I thought perhaps you were teaching Jennifer about tying knots.'

'Knots?'

'You must have noticed how whenever there's a lady on board the pirate boat, the Pirate Captain will always disappear into his cabin with her for a while, and afterwards, when any of us ask what they were doing, he tells us he was just teaching the lady how to tie knots, because most girls don't know much about nautical matters. Between you and me, I think he must tell funny anecdotes at the same time as showing them how to tie knots, because quite often I've heard a lot of giggling. But that's not to say the Captain doesn't take his knot tying seriously—he obviously puts a lot of effort into it, as he tends to come out from a knot-tying lesson looking quite exhausted.'

The pirate with a scarf wondered if it were perhaps time to sit down with some of the crew and set them straight on a couple of matters.

'So eventually I decided to follow you into the tent myself,' continued the pirate with an accordion. 'But you were nowhere to be seen! It was completely empty, except for a half-used-up bottle of chloroform. I looked about for a while, and then I found there was a trapdoor hidden in the floor, which led to some steps. And the steps led to a creepy-looking tunnel. Well, that all seemed rather rum. I think it was part of an old sewer system, and you know how you're always reading about people flushing away baby alligators which then grow to gigantic proportions, so—given that alligators

and us pirates have got a bit of a troubled history—I was pretty frightened, but I played the most upbeat shanties I could think of to keep myself calm. The tunnel went on for a few hundred yards, and then I got to more stairs, lots of them this time, and they led up here. Now I've found you I suppose I should probably—'

But without saying another word, the pirate with an accordion died of scurvy, right there and then.

'Blast,' said Erasmus.

'I wasn't expecting that,' said Jennifer miserably.

'Idiot!' said the pirate with a scarf. 'I told him what would happen if he just ate candy all the time instead of limes.'

Scurvy Jake and the Pirate Captain had gone on signing autographs for most of the afternoon. Occasionally the Pirate Captain got a bit annoyed to hear Scurvy Jake passing off one of the Pirate Captain's exciting anecdotes as if it were his own, but he decided to let it slide. After they had both run out of photographs—the Pirate Captain was pleased to have pocketed over sixty doubloons for his efforts—they decided to wander over to the part of the convention where several stalls were selling piratical equipment at trade prices. There was a lot of good-natured bargaining going on, as pirates jostled each other for the best deals. The Pirate Captain picked up a job lot of thirty portholes for just twenty-eight pounds—less than a pound per porthole! He also bought a barrel of tar, six bottles of Pirate Rum, and a few tricorn hats just to spite everybody. Satisfied with his purchases, he and Scurvy Jake headed over to the Metropolitan's bar to drink and reminisce.

Pretty soon Scurvy Jake was a bit worse the wear from all the grog.

'I was a terrible pirate,' he said in a cracked voice. 'You were always a much better pirate than me.'

It was true, thought the Pirate Captain. Scurvy Jake had always been a rubbish pirate. With his lumbering lack of coordination and his giant hands, he was no good at tying knots, and he was famous for repeatedly burying treasure and then forgetting where he'd left it. But the Pirate Captain didn't like to see his old friend upset.

'Pfft! I've made a few mistakes myself,' said the Pirate Captain, trying to console him. 'Like that time I let a cannibal join the crew. And that other time when I said, "Well, I don't see any hurricane." I'm not perfect.'

'But I'm the worst pirate ever. I'm so clumsy,' sobbed Scurvy Jake.

'What about Courteous Frank? He was easily a worse pirate than you ever were. I heard he refused to let his crew cure the ship's meat with salt, because he'd read that a high sodium intake had been linked to heart disease. Died eating a slice of rancid ham. You're not even close!'

'It's kind of you to say so, Pirate Captain. You know, if there's anything I can do to help, you just have to ask. Are you on holiday, or are you on an adventure?'

'Adventure. And you can help, Scurvy Jake!' The Pirate Captain's beard glittered with piratical cunning. 'Do you know where I could get hold of a big white sheet?'

Eleven

MAROONED!

'He's not just evil! He's insane! A one hundred per cent Grade-A lunatic!' shouted Darwin, flinging the evening edition of the *Mail* at the Pirate Captain, who had returned from his Pirate Convention and was helping set up the stage of the Natural History Museum's lecture room for the evening's performance. 'The Bishop of Oxford has persisted with his ridiculous scare-mongering. Now he's saying that if I go ahead with my Man-panzee demonstration, the Holy Ghost—the Holy Ghost!—will personally make an appearance at my lecture, and wrestle me and Mister Bobo to the ground! Really, it's too much!'

'It's not the Bishop's work. It's mine,' said the Pirate Captain, chewing the end off a fat cigar, and looking smug. Sometimes the Pirate Captain found himself thinking what a fantastic, hard-bitten, and wily newspaper mogul he would have made, had he not taken up piracy instead. Darwin slumped into one of the auditorium's seats.

'I'm not sure I follow,' he said weakly.

'I'm the one who started the rumour. And—even though I say it myself—it's a stroke of genius.'

'For pity's sake, why?'

'Listen, Charles. You've got a lot to learn about this science business. It's not all about test tubes and creatures and bits of gauze.'

'It isn't?'

'No, it isn't. The whole thing became clear to me when I was talking to an old friend of mine. He was telling me how great at pirating he always thought I was,' explained the Pirate Captain. 'And the fact is, I have made something of a name for myself in nautical circles. But why do you think that is?'

Darwin scratched his head thoughtfully. 'Your luxuriant beard?'

'Aaarrr,' said the Pirate Captain. 'That probably plays a part in it. But more than that, I think it's because of my gift for showmanship. Like the way I drink rum mixed with gunpowder, even though it tastes disgusting. And the way I run people through in such a grisly manner.'

'Surely,' said Darwin, 'it's not possible to be run through in any manner other than a grisly one?'

'Now, a lot of people will tell you that. But it's not the case. You take the pirate with a scarf. He's such a proficient swordsman that I've seen him run a man through without spilling a drop of blood,* and the fellow on the receiving end dies in a speedy and humane fashion. Me, on the other hand, I'm forever making a mess of it, hacking about all over the shop, getting my cutlass stuck in a particularly tough bit of gristle. Yet, quite inadvertently, this has all added to my fearsome reputation! And with pirating, reputation is everything.'

'I'm *still* not sure I follow you,' said the puzzled young scientist.

'Mister Bobo is a fantastic achievement. But there's a thousand other scientists out there trying to make a name for themselves. So if you're going to stand out and impress the stony-faced Victorian establishment, you need a gimmick! A bit of controversy! It's all about the presentation.'

So the Pirate Captain explained his latest plan. Though perhaps it was a little more complicated than his usual plans, which tended

*There are roughly eight pints of blood in the average human. Blood contains red cells, white cells, and platelets suspended in a proteinacious fluid called plasma. The first dog biscuit to be made entirely out of blood was invented by Tamsin Virgo, a young woman from Stoke, England.

to involve how much ham to eat, the Pirate Captain was confident of success. Darwin was less certain.

'I don't know, Pirate Captain,' he said with a sad shake of his head, once the Captain had finished. 'It all seems such a risk. This lecture is expressly against the Bishop's wishes. I can't help but think something truly terrible will befall my poor brother.'

'Well, I'm in the same boat myself,' said the Pirate Captain with a shrug. 'Two of my pirates never returned from investigating that sinister circus. There's a good chance the Bishop has some evil fate planned for them too. I'm not really that bothered about the swab with the accordion, but that other fellow . . . the one with a scarf'—the Pirate Captain really never seemed to be able to remember the names of any of his crew—'the truth is, I'm at a bit of a loss without him. He cleans my hats, keeps me up-to-date with all the latest shanties, and he even knows all the proper nautical terms for things. I bet you didn't realise that on a sailing boat you're not even meant to say "upstairs" or "downstairs" or "left" or "right". It's all "port" this and "starboard" that and "galley" instead of kitchen and goodness knows what else. How am I expected to remember that kind of thing? Anyhow. What was the point I was making?'

'I'm not really sure,' said Darwin.

'Well then,' said the Pirate Captain, flashing the scientist his most winning grin.

The Royal Society's grandfather clock struck a quarter past ten. It was just a few minutes to go until Darwin's big moment, and the lecture hall was fast filling up. Most of the audience had read the evening papers' controversial headlines, and there was an excited buzz of anticipation throughout the room. The Pirate Captain's ploy had certainly done the trick in bringing in the crowds, thought Darwin. He stood at the door, greeting people as they arrived, whilst Mister Bobo paced backstage taking nervous swigs from a flask of whisky.

'Nice that you could make it. Hi. Hello. Thanks for coming. Glad you could be here. Nice to—'

Darwin froze. He found himself face-to-face with the Bishop of Oxford.

'Darwin.'

'Bishop.'

'So you're going ahead with this?'

'I—uh—that is . . . it looks that way.'

'What a pity your brother Erasmus couldn't be here.'

'You villain! What have you done with him?'

'Mr Darwin . . . Charles. I haven't the slightest clue what you're talking about. I just hope his health isn't suffering,' said the Bishop, waggling his bushy brows and grimacing to show that he meant the exact opposite of what he was saying. 'It's not too late to reconsider,' he added as he took his seat in the audience, unwittingly right next to the Pirate Captain, who was back in scientist disguise.

The lights dimmed, the thick velvet curtain went up, and Darwin and Mister Bobo came out to enormous applause.

'Ladies and gentlemen. He's hairy! He's scary! I would like to introduce you to the world's first fantastic . . . Man-panzee!'

The spotlight fell on Mister Bobo, who was so well turned out, with his hair slicked back, a breath mint in his mouth, and his best dress shirt tucked into a pair of handsome trousers, that it looked like he was going on a first date. In actual fact, Mister Bobo had never so much as kissed a girl. The audience clapped again. Darwin coughed nervously, and started to explain how he fed Mister Bobo on a diet of pituitary glands taken from the cadavers of baby seals.

'One might expect the pituitary gland to have some effect on the language capabilities of the simian brain, but I can't detect any. Mister Bobo just seems to like the taste,' said Darwin.

Ker-chunk!

The gigantic cog clicked on another notch.

'Shall we have a game of animal, vegetable, or mineral? To take our minds off things?' suggested Erasmus brightly. The scarf-wearing pirate would have enjoyed a game of hangman more, but seeing as they didn't have any chalk, and their hands were all tied up anyhow, he nodded reluctantly.

'I'll go first,' said the pirate. 'Okay, I've thought of something.'

'Are you a mineral?' asked Erasmus.

'Nope.'

'Animal?'

'Sort of.'

'Sort of?'

'All right, yes. Animal.'

'Are you a hoofed animal?'

'No.'

'Claws?'

'No.'

'Not claws or hoofs? What does that leave? Trotters?'

'Yes!'

'So you're a pig?'

'Not exactly . . .'

'Not exactly a pig? Then a bit of a pig? Are you bacon?'

'No, but you're getting warm.'

'Ham?'

'That's it! I'm a succulent piece of ham! But you took too many guesses, so I won, and I get to choose again.'

Darwin had finished his introduction and explanation of his training methods, and now he was leading Mister Bobo—who was doing his best not to knuckle-walk, because he knew just how vulgar that

looked—over to a carefully laid out dinner table in the centre of the stage.

'Mister Bobo—would you be so kind as to show these ladies and gentlemen exactly which of these spoons you would use to eat a dessert?'

Mister Bobo held up the correct spoon almost instantly, and the audience let out some 'oohs' and 'aahs'. His confidence building, Mister Bobo proceeded to run through the rest of the routine with aplomb. Shown pictures of two different girls, he correctly identified which one was more attractive, he made a selection of cocktails called out by the audience, and he played 'God Save the Queen' and 'Crockett's Theme' on the piano, without hitting a single wrong note.

Ker-chunk!

'So you're not actually a cow?' said Jennifer, rolling her eyes in exasperation.

'No,' grinned the pirate with a scarf.

'Are you a steak?'

'No!'

'I give up.'

'I'm a sausage! But one made out of beef instead of pork. Right—I've thought of something else!'

'Is this going to be meat-based again?'

'It might be.'

Darwin and Mister Bobo were building up to the grand finale. The lecture had gone well, and the audience seemed politely impressed, but it clearly needed something more to whip them into a frenzy.

With a prearranged signal from Mister Bobo, a clattering noise came from offstage, and then a lumbering figure appeared.

'Wait a minute! Who's this?' said Darwin, looking surprised. 'Oh my goodness! Ladies and Gentlemen . . . it's the Holy Ghost!'

'Wooo! Raaah!' said the Holy Ghost, a bit muffled, sounding a lot like Scurvy Jake with a sheet over his head. There was the plink-plink of gentlemen dropping monocles into their drinks and the gentle rustle of several ladies fainting.

'He's come to get me, because my theories are so blasphemous!' shouted Darwin, in mock terror. Nobody noticed the twinkle in his eye. 'The Holy Ghost is attacking me! Look at the Holy Ghost!'

'Rah!' said the Holy Ghost, in a booming voice. 'The science you are doing is too shocking by half! I've come to wrestle you! I will lay the smackdown on your wicked ways!'

Gasps shot round the auditorium, and Darwin was pleased to see he had the audience on the edge of their seats. He just had time to notice the Pirate Captain lean over to the Bishop and whisper something in his ear, before his attention was diverted by the Holy Ghost picking him up and hurling the young scientist straight through the middle of the dining table.*

'Dear me! The actual Holy Ghost!' the Pirate Captain was saying to his neighbour. 'If I'd done any sins, I'd probably want to get them off my chest right about now. Like that time I kidnapped somebody. I'm really sorry about that. What about you, Bishop? Have you ever done any sins? Like kidnapping?'

'That's not the Holy Ghost,' snorted the Bishop dismissively.

'Yes it is!' said the Pirate Captain, a bit put out. 'Look how tall he is! He's a giant! And he's covered in a big sheet! Just like it describes him in the Bible.'

*Wrestlers today are highly trained professionals, and obviously you should never try smacking people about the head with chairs or throwing them through tables at home. Even the best wrestlers get injured—Mick Foley, three times WWF champion, has broken most of the bones in his body during his career, lost several teeth and even an ear.

'The Bible says nothing of the kind. Where on earth did you get the idea that the Holy Ghost is a giant? He's the same size as Jesus. That's the point—he's just a creepier version of Christ.'

'Are you sure?' frowned the Captain, wondering if his research had let him down. 'Doesn't he fight Goliath at some point? I'm sure he does. He throws a leper at his face.'

'No. I've no idea where you've picked all this up from.'

'It's just after the bit where he hides in that gigantic wooden horse. Isn't it?'

'I think you're a trifle confused.'

'Ah well. Plan B,' said the Pirate Captain with a disappointed shrug. He whipped his cutlass out from under his lab coat and jabbed it in the Bishop's ribs. 'I'm not really a scientist—I'm the Pirate Captain! Tell me what you've done with Erasmus!'

The Bishop didn't miss a beat. 'Why! Look over there! Is that a treasure chest?' he said.

Even though he knew better, the Pirate Captain looked over to where the Bishop was pointing. The villain took this opportunity to bolt from the lecture room. 'I just can't help myself,' thought the Pirate Captain irritably. 'Damn my piratical nature!'

He leapt to his feet, pulled off the cumbersome lab coat, and, seeing the stricken look on Darwin's face, gave the scientist a reassuring thumbs-up to show he had it all under control. Then the Pirate Captain chased as fast as he could after the despicable cleric, pausing only briefly to give his card to a striking blonde sitting in the second row.

Darwin, having little option but to hope the Pirate Captain knew what he was doing, went on hamming it up as he pretended to be desperately trying to make a wrestling tag with Mister Bobo. After a great deal of gurning and grunting he slapped the monkey's hand, and Mister Bobo leapt into centre stage and swung a folding metal chair at the head of the Holy Ghost, who promptly collapsed in a heap. Darwin held up Mister Bobo's hand triumphantly.

'Hooray for science!' he shouted. 'Tell your friends! Tell your

family! And don't forget that Mister Bobo merchandise can be purchased from the museum shop!'

And with that, the audience were on their feet, giving Darwin a spectacular thunderous ovation.

The Pirate Captain skidded to a halt in the museum's cavernous main hall, realised he had lost sight of the fleeing Bishop, and said a terrible salty pirate oath. It occurred to him that the Bishop might be hiding inside the gigantic armadillo shell that was one of the Pirate Captain's favourite exhibits, but before he could check it out he was alerted by a scuffling sound from the balcony above, and so he began to charge up the marble staircase, four steps at a time, only to find an enormous slice of California redwood* rolling straight towards him. A full twenty feet in diameter, the redwood came within a whisker of crushing the Pirate Captain flat, but he just managed to dive out of the way with an athletic leap. The monstrous redwood still knocked off his pirate hat though.

'That's my favourite hat, Bishop! You're not doing yourself any favours!'

The Pirate Captain bounded to the top of the stairs and saw the Bishop disappearing into the Hall of Fossils. Waving his cutlass and roaring, for effect more than anything, he careered inside, and almost found himself smashed in the face by a trilobite. The Bishop had a whole armful of trilobites and was flinging them at the Pirate Captain like prehistoric discuses. The Captain did his best to bat them away with his cutlass.

'Stop throwing trilobites at me!' shouted the Pirate Captain, because it was the only thing he could think of to say, given the situation. Luckily for the Pirate Captain they were not having their climactic

*The California redwood is the biggest and most majestic tree in the world. Some of them can grow as high as 367 feet (13 London buses) and as broad as 22 feet in diameter (4/5 of a London bus). Their flowers are cones and they can live for over 2,000 years.

fight in Prague Natural History Museum, which is full of trilobites and not much else, and the Bishop quickly exhausted his supply of fossils. He dashed into the adjoining room, and the Pirate Captain followed at full tilt, even though it contained the museum's collection of stuffed birds, which the Pirate Captain had always found especially creepy.

The Bishop swung a dodo at the advancing pirate, sending his cutlass flying. In return the Pirate Captain picked up an albatross and flung it squarely at the Bishop.

'Ooof!' said the Bishop, his mouth full of albatross wing. He clambered onto a balustrade and leapt from the balcony. For a moment the Pirate Captain thought the Bishop had decided to end it all, but then he realised that the wily cleric had landed on the skull of the enormous brontosaurus that was the museum's centrepiece, and was now sprinting down its bony neck to safety. The Pirate Captain jumped over the balcony himself and decided to slide down the skeleton's neck like it was a banister on the pirate boat, a decision he pretty quickly regretted. It took a moment for him to get his breath back and for his eyes to stop watering, by which time the Bishop had fled into the Mineral Room. The room's curator was surprised to see anybody coming into the Mineral Room, arguably the most boring room in the whole museum, let alone the Bishop of Oxford hotly pursued by an angry-looking pirate.

The Bishop smashed open a display case, sending a cloud of dust into the air, and flung a hefty rock at the Pirate Captain. The Pirate Captain squinted—it looked like a piece of iron as it hurtled towards his luxuriant beard. Moving lightning fast the Pirate Captain scanned the display in front of him, found a big chunk of nickel, and hurled it back towards the Bishop. The nickel hit the iron and knocked it into a thousand splinters.

'Ha!' cried the Pirate Captain. 'Nickel! Atomic weight 58.69—beats your iron, atomic weight 55.85. In your face, Bishop!'

'So let's see you deal with this!' shouted the Bishop, hefting a lump of ruthenium at the pirate.

'Ruthenium! Atomic weight 101.07! Goodness me!' cried the Pirate Captain, though perhaps in slightly saltier terms than that. He barely found a slab of osmium—atomic weight 190.2—in time.

Several elements later they were still deadlocked, and fast running out of periodic table.*

'Give up, Bishop!' said the Pirate Captain, a nugget of selenium whizzing past his ear.

'Oh, give up yourself!' shouted the Bishop, unimaginatively.

The Pirate Captain was momentarily put off when he picked up a lump of what he took to be gold, before realising it was actually iron pyrite—fool's gold, the dreaded nemesis of pirates everywhere—and his pause gave the Bishop an opportunity to escape the Mineral Room and head into the Hall of Mammals. The Pirate Captain charged after him relentlessly, but the Bishop had managed to snap the tusk off a shabby-looking walrus, and as the two men grappled he slowly inched his makeshift weapon towards the Pirate Captain's neck. The Bishop was unexpectedly strong.

'Do you work out?' asked the Pirate Captain through gritted teeth.

'A little,' said the Bishop, his face turning red. 'And yourself?'

'When I have the chance.'

'What do you bench-press?' hissed the Bishop.

'Around a hundred and ten pounds. How about you?'

'Oh . . . a hundred and twenty . . . hundred and twenty-five . . . or thereabouts.'

'Damn.'

The trouble, reflected the Pirate Captain, was that the pirate boat's gym was covered in mirrors, so whenever he worked out he would glimpse himself pulling a ridiculously strained face, which just made

*Mendeleyev is widely credited as being the first person to produce a 'periodic table of the elements' in 1869, but that, you'll notice, is a full thirty years after these events are supposed to be taking place. I leave readers to draw their own conclusions.

him laugh and not be able to take it all that seriously. As a result he had failed to keep up with the weights regime that had been set out for him by the pirate who was a jock. But he was paying for it now. The Pirate Captain genuinely thought he was done for. The tusk pressed against his throat, cutting off his pirate breath, and as consciousness began to slip away the Pirate Captain felt like he was starting to hallucinate—it seemed as if the very exhibits behind the Bishop were writhing and coming alive! Then he realised that the exhibit behind the Bishop really *was* moving. A hairy arm reached out, there was the distinct sound of monkey fist smashing into bishop skull, and the Bishop of Oxford collapsed in a daze. The walrus tusk clattered to the floor, and the Pirate Captain looked up to see that what he had taken to be part of the stuffed chimpanzee display was actually Mister Bobo!

'Thanks for that, Mister Bobo,' said the Pirate Captain breathlessly, shaking him by the hand.

AAARGH! | ME | BEAUTIES! said Mister Bobo with his cards, laughing a monkey laugh.

Twelve

SWINGING FROM THE YARDARM!

Darwin helped the Pirate Captain to his feet, and gave him back his hat.

'It's a good job I cut that question and answer session short,' he said. 'Looks like me and Mister Bobo only just got here in time.'

'No need,' said the Pirate Captain, gingerly rubbing his neck. 'I had the fiend just where I wanted him.'

'You'd started to turn blue.'

'Aaarrr. It's an old pirate trick,' said the Pirate Captain defensively. 'Not something lubbers would understand. But enough about me—how did the lecture go?'

'It was fantastic!' said Darwin with a big grin. 'I got five phone numbers from pretty girls! Five!' He waved some scraps of perfumed paper at the Pirate Captain. 'They couldn't get enough of Mister Bobo! And you were right, when he smashed that chair over the Holy Ghost's head, they almost jumped out of their seats! I'm sure they'll go home and tell everyone how shocking it all was, and how science is in the infernal pocket of Lucifer, but secretly they loved it. I've been invited to do a tour of the American universities! And Mister Bobo is going to appear on the cover of *Nature*.'

Mister Bobo gave a sheepish shrug, but you could tell he was pleased.

'Look, shall we grab a coffee?' asked Darwin. 'My shout. I've got to tell you all about the bit when I thought Scurvy Jake was actually going to sit on my head!'

'I rather think we should find out what this wretch has done with your missing brother first,' said the Pirate Captain, giving the Bishop a quick kick in the gut.

'Erasmus!' Darwin slapped his uncommonly large forehead with his palm. 'In all the excitement I'd clean forgot!'

The young scientist knelt down and shook the dazed Bishop by his bushy sideburns. 'Where is he? What have you done with my brother, you brute? I'll cut your pretty face!'

'No! Not the face!' cried the Bishop, holding up his hands to protect his beautiful skin. 'He's tied to a big cog inside Big Ben! But you're much too late—as soon as Big Ben chimes midnight, he'll get another cog right in the chops!'

The unlikely trio hurried down to Parliament Square.

'Look! Only twenty minutes to go! How are we ever going to reach them in time?!' wailed Darwin.

'Aaarrr,' said the Pirate Captain, because he couldn't think of anything more helpful to say.

Darwin tried to look resolute. 'Climbing! It's the only way. One of us will have to climb up there!'

Big Ben loomed forbiddingly out of the fog. The Pirate Captain craned his neck, and felt a bit ill just looking up at the towering clock.

'Oh, well,' he shrugged. 'I'm afraid us pirates are notoriously rubbish at climbing up tall buildings. It's like that old shanty says . . . if a-climbing you need to go, leave those pirates down below, they're no good at it yo ho ho . . .'

It sounded to Darwin suspiciously like the Pirate Captain was making this shanty up as he went along.

'What about monkeys? They're always climbing up tall buildings! How about it Mister Bobo?' said the Pirate Captain, giving him an encouraging slap on his hairy back.

Mister Bobo chose his flash cards carefully.

[NO] [F*!$%NG] [WAY] signed the monkey.

'Well, Charles. It *is* your brother.'

Darwin squinted at the distant clock face and shivered.

'Ah . . . you know, me and Erasmus were never that close. He was a very solitary child. Not much of a brother at all.'

But Mister Bobo was holding up his cards again.

[WHAT] [ABOUT] [FITZROY] [AND] [HIS] [AIRSHIP?] he spelt out.

'Ah-ha!' cried the Pirate Captain. 'The little *panpongidae* fellow has it! We could steal the airship, pop it with my cutlass, and fashion a big rope from all the silk!'

'Or we could float up there in the airship. Because it's an airship.'

'Yes. Yes, we could do that instead. Either way's good. I'm not bothered.'

They hailed an olden-days taxi—which back in those topsy-turvy times used horses instead of electricity—and hurried back to South Kensington as fast as they could. Sprinting into the Natural History Museum, the Pirate Captain quickly grabbed his men, who he found in the gift shop buying dinosaur masks and roaring at each other.*

'Raagh!' roared a pirate. 'I'm a triceratops!'

'Grraagh! I'm a brontosaurus!'

It was like the usual pirate roaring, but even better. They all stopped and paid attention when the Pirate Captain burst in.

'Stop mucking about, pirates!' he shouted. 'We've got a bit of traditional pirate boarding to do!'

*To this day one of the best things you can buy in the Natural History Museum gift shop is a lenticular dinosaur ruler. When you waggle it back and forth, the dinosaurs appear to attack each other in an exciting fashion.

The pirates all flung off their scientist disguises, but several of them kept on their dinosaur masks because they figured it made them look even more fearsome than they already were. Into the gentlemen's club they charged.

'Dino-pirates!' cried a scientist, dropping his pipe in surprise. 'It's my worst nightmare!'

The Pirate Captain waved his pirate cutlass at FitzRoy and Glaisher, the airship scientist, who were sitting in a corner arguing over what the best bit about being a meteorologist was.

'It's the clouds,' FitzRoy was saying. 'Clouds are easily the best bit about meteorology.'

'Nonsense!' said Glaisher. 'It's the barometers.'

'We're boarding your airship!' bellowed the Pirate Captain. 'Prepare to be overrun! By pirates!'

FitzRoy and his friend reluctantly took the pirates round the back of the museum, to where the airship was parked. Its enormous gasbag billowed in the wind, attached by a series of sturdy ropes to a luxurious-looking gondola. The pirates all clambered aboard.

'I think this may be a first. We're taking pirating into a whole new era. They'll probably put us on stamps,' whispered the Pirate Captain to the pirate dressed in green.

'How does it float?' asked Darwin, turning to FitzRoy and Glaisher and pulling a face to show how sorry he was to be responsible for the pirates stealing their beloved airship.

'Initially we used helium as the lifting agent,' replied FitzRoy with a grimace. 'But it turned out to have a terrible and dangerous flaw.'

'Which was?'

'The pilots were always so busy larking about with the gas cylinders, making their voices go all squeaky, that they kept on smashing into trees and buildings.* So now I've switched to hydrogen. I can't

*Much like bananas, supplies of helium may also run out within the next twenty years. Helium is not just used in party balloons, it is also important for the manufacture of superconductors.

see any sort of dangerous flaw when it comes to good old reliable hydrogen,' said the young captain, moving several boxes of fireworks out of the way so that he could get to the steering wheel.

'It's certainly impressive. You can tell no expense has been spared. I like what you've done with that roaring log fire next to those spare cylinders of hydrogen in the lounge,' said the Pirate Captain politely as they wandered about the gondola.

FitzRoy, busy throwing out ballast and letting loose the anchor rope, though annoyed to find himself being hijacked by pirates for the second time in the space of one adventure, still appreciated their compliments nonetheless.

'Be sure to check out the splendid smokers' gallery,' he said. 'You'll find it affords tremendous views of the billowing bags of hydrogen gas. And help yourself to the chops which are cooking on the airship's flaming barbecue.'

After some chops, the pirates all helped to shovel coal into the blazing furnace that powered the airship's engines.

'It's a lot quicker than a boat,' said the pirate in green appreciatively, once they were airborne.

'And that scientist is right. You *can* see down ladies' tops. Look!' exclaimed the albino pirate excitedly.

'I think I like this better than sailing. You don't get wet, and I haven't been sick once,' said the pirate who chain-smoked, lighting his cigarette and tossing away the match.

'It does have its drawbacks, mind,' cautioned FitzRoy. The albino pirate was just about to ask what sort of drawbacks there could possibly be when a low-flying crow smacked right into his face. FitzRoy sighed and shook his head sadly.

Above the ever-present fog they could see the dim lights of the city stretching out in all directions. The dirigible bobbed across central London at quite a rate, and soon they had Big Ben in sight. The Pirate Captain did a pirate gob on one of the tourists below, and was pleased to see his aim was still good.

'Heavens to Betsy!' cried Darwin. 'We've only got three minutes! We haven't time to try to find purchase on the roof. One of us will have to jump across!'

There was the unmistakable sound of several pirates staring at their fingernails.

'Honestly!' bellowed the Pirate Captain, very disappointed at his lads. 'I've been attacked by jellyfish with more backbone than you lot! Well, then. If none of you lubbers will volunteer, we'll just have to settle this the old pirate way.'

The crew looked deathly serious—the Pirate Captain could mean only one thing!

A few moments later the albino pirate took a deep breath, counted to three, and held out his clenched fist. He tried to look apologetic, but a big grin spread all across his face.

'Sorry, Captain. Pirate stone blunts your pirate scissors.'

'Whatever,' said the Pirate Captain tetchily, thinking for a moment about trying to pretend that the two fingers he was holding up were actually supposed to represent a narrow piece of paper rather than a pair of scissors. But ancient pirate tradition was ancient pirate tradition, and there was no use arguing with it. He bent down to make sure his bootlaces were done up, checked he had as big a run-up as possible, let out a mighty roar, and leapt the gap between the airship and Big Ben.

The Pirate Captain had been expecting to smash right through the gigantic glass clock face, thereby making one of his famously dramatic entrances, but he just slapped against it with a sound like a side of beef hitting a chopping board, and slowly began to slide down in a daze. Luckily the Pirate Captain had the presence of mind to grab at the huge cast-iron minute hand, and there he hung, his

coattails flapping. He took a deep breath to relax himself, but the buffeting winds were doing nothing to calm his nerves and even though he didn't mean to, he glanced down. The people on the streets below looked just like ants, thought the Pirate Captain, but not regular ants, more like some kind of sinister super-ants that wore clothes and hats and carried newspapers instead of bits of leaf. Noticing the worried looks on his crew's faces as they leant anxiously out of the airship's gondola, he felt like he ought to make some sort of wisecrack in an effort to look hard-boiled and nonchalant, possibly involving a play on words with 'time', something like: 'I'm not having the TIME of my life!' But he didn't, he just grimaced a bit instead. With an effort he managed to twist himself about, and give one of the glass panels in the clock face a big kick. To the Pirate Captain's relief the panel shattered with the first blow, and after some grunting and sucking in of his gut, he was able to clamber inside.

The Pirate Captain rushed over to help Jennifer first, because she was the prettiest. He hefted the top off the big glass tube and helped her climb out. Jennifer flung her arms round his sturdy shoulders.

'Thanks! I thought I was going to end up as a bar of soap for sure! My name is Jennifer.'

'And I'm the Pirate Captain. It's a pleasure to meet you.'

'Likewise.'

'I have my own pirate boat, you know.'

'Really?'

'It has twelve cannons.'

'Goodness! That's a lot of cannons. Your beard is fantastic, by the way.'

'That's nice of you to say so. You yourself have a lovely face.'

'Oh! You're sweet.'

'Us pirates aren't just the weather-beaten rogues we're portrayed as. We have a soft side too. Also, my boat has silk sheets.'

There was a sudden sickening crunch of metal against bone, and an alarmed yelp. The Pirate Captain pulled a guilty face and slapped his forgetful forehead. He rushed over to the gigantic cog and dragged Erasmus Darwin from between its monstrous teeth.

'Sorry about that,' said the Pirate Captain with an apologetic grin. 'I'd forget my own head if it wasn't nailed down.'

'Oh! My arm!' wailed Erasmus.

'Aaarrr. Let's not get too precious about an arm,' said the Captain. 'Some of my crew don't even have legs! Just little wooden pegs. I swear, half of them are more like chairs than pirates!'*

The Pirate Captain began to untie the ropes attaching the pirate with a scarf to the huge cog.

'I wish you wouldn't get yourself into trouble like this,' he scolded his trusty number two. But he meant it in an affectionate manner. You could tell this because when the Pirate Captain scolded somebody in a manner that wasn't affectionate they tended to end up with a cutlass in their belly. 'You're definitely the best one out of my whole crew. You're worth ten of any of the rest of them'—the Pirate Captain paused and fought back a grin—'because you have so many gold teeth!'

The pirate with a scarf laughed. The Pirate Captain always made that exact same joke, but they both knew that he really would be sorry to see anything happen to his able second in command. For a start, without help from the scarf-wearing pirate, the Pirate Captain probably wouldn't have remembered where they had left the boat. And even though the pirate with a scarf knew that he really should be disappointed by the looks Jennifer was now giving his debonair captain, for some reason he mostly just felt relieved. When it came down to it, he was much more comfortable thinking about scarves and pirating than he was thinking about ladies.

---

*Loss of limbs was an occupational hazard for pirates. As a result most ships offered a degree of compensation for pirates injured in battle. Loss of an eye would net you 100 pieces of eight, loss of a right arm 600 pieces of eight, and loss of a left leg 400 pieces of eight.

The Pirate Captain turned to give Darwin, FitzRoy, and the rest of the pirates bobbing about in the dirigible a wave through the shattered bit of clock face to show them that everything was fine, and in the process almost tripped over the pirate with an accordion, who was sprawled across the floor.

'What's up with *this* swab?' asked the Pirate Captain, nudging him with the toe of his shiny pirate boot.

'He died of scurvy, sir,' said the pirate with a scarf.

'Aaaarrr. I hope that's proved a useful lesson to you. Ham is all well and good, but make sure you get your vitamins! Scurvy is no laughing matter,' said the Pirate Captain. 'Except in those rare instances when a fellow's head swells up like a gigantic lemon,' he added as an afterthought. 'Which I grant can bring a smile even to my salty old face.'

Thirteen

TO THE PIRATE COAST!

'. . . seven . . . eight . . . nine. Nine hams. Nine juicy hams.'

The Pirate Captain made a note on his clipboard. 'Well, that's just about everything.'

The pirates were back in Littlehampton Docks, and they had just finished loading up the pirate boat with fresh supplies of meat and grog. The only thing that remained to be wheeled on board was the pirate with an accordion, whom the other pirates had decided to have stuffed and nickel-plated, because they thought it was what he would have wanted, and besides which the pirate boat could never have too many lucky mascots. Jennifer, whom the Pirate Captain had made an honorary pirate, reckoned it was a bit on the creepy side, but pirates were a superstitious bunch.*

Darwin, Erasmus, and Mister Bobo had come down to wave them off. Darwin was almost unrecognisable from the callow

*There are several seafaring superstitions. It is widely believed that redheads bring bad luck to a ship, though this can be averted if you speak to the redhead before they speak to you. Flat-footed people are also considered best avoided, as is dark-coloured luggage.

youth the Pirate Captain had first met on this adventure—he had started to grow a little beard, his clothes were of the best Savile Row cut, and he had his arms round two vivacious-looking brunettes.

'Good luck then, Charles. I hope all the science goes well,' said the Pirate Captain, shaking him warmly by the hand.

'I think I'm really getting the hang of it,' said Darwin eagerly. 'I've got a lot more ideas to keep the audience on their toes. I'm going to fit a soundproofed box in the corner of my lecture theatres where I'll invite scientists too frightened to hear the shocking conclusion to my nightmarish theories to sit out the rest of the talk. And I'm offering life insurance policies to everybody in case my terrifying ideas scare them to death. I'm trying to work out a way to make all the seats vibrate. I'm calling it "Evolvovision". Me and Mister Bobo are going to be the smash hit of Victorian science—and I owe it all to you and your pirates, Pirate Captain!'

'Aaarrrr! Don't mention it! It's been a pleasure,' said the Pirate Captain. 'I have to say, when I first saw you, I thought—there's a man whose face isn't really big enough for the size of his head. But you've proved me wrong. Oh, and by the way . . .'

The Pirate Captain paused.

'Indian, North Pacific, South Pacific, Antarctic, Arctic, North Atlantic, South Atlantic. I'm not a complete idiot, you know.'

The pirate boat slowly pulled out of the shabby dock, and all the pirates waved the steadily shrinking trio goodbye. The Pirate Captain smiled. There were good bits about the land, he reflected, like the shops and the way it didn't wobble about all the time, but he'd missed the ocean. The Pirate Captain actually became quite lost in his thoughts about how much he liked the crashing waves and seaweed and being a pirate and that, until an indignant cough jolted him back to the moment.

'And what do you propose to do with me?' said the Bishop of Oxford, who had been lashed to the boat's mast.

'We'll find an uninhabited island someplace,' said the Pirate Captain, 'and then we'll maroon you. It's the pirate way.'

'I don't much like the sound of that.'

'Oh, it's not so bad. For some reason Pirate Law says you're allowed to take a few records. And the odd book. I think it's eight of each.'

'Can I take the Bible?'

'Oh, you get that anyway. And the complete works of Shakespeare. But the rest is up to you. Don't be clever and choose *Robinson Crusoe*—everybody does that.'

The Pirate Captain turned back to watch Littlehampton's amusement arcade fade into the distance.

'That went pretty well, don't you think, number two?' he said to the pirate with a scarf.

'Yes, Captain. Though maybe our next adventure should be a little less episodic? And not be so confusing at times?' said the pirate with a scarf, leaning on the boat's safety railings and enjoying the spray of the sea on his face.

'Aaargh. You're right. And towards the last half of this adventure, I don't know if you noticed, but we stopped having half as many feasts. That was a pity.'

'And we didn't really end up with much treasure,' said the albino pirate sadly. 'Which is usually the best bit about our adventures.'

'Oh, I didn't come away completely empty-handed,' said the Pirate Captain with a grin. He rummaged about in the silky folds of his beard, where, amongst the ribbons and the luxuriant hair, something shiny seemed to be lodged. The Captain eventually prised it free. He held up a large nugget of metal. It gleamed white in the evening sun, and the pirate with a scarf whistled in admiration.

'Ruthenium!' said the albino pirate.

'Aaargh. That it is. Atomic number forty-four. Most valuable metal in the world.* Better than gold—and you know how highly I rate gold, so that's saying something.'

All the pirate crew cheered their captain, and then they went downstairs to do some shantying.

And with that, the pirate boat sailed about for a bit.

*Ruthenium is one of the ultrarare 'Platinum Group metals'. It has a melting point of 2310°C and a boiling point of 3900°C, 44 protons, 44 electrons, and 57 neutrons.

COMPREHENSION EXERCISE

Answer all questions to the best of your abilities

1. What do you think the themes of this book were? Several commentators have described the main theme as 'pirates'. Another theme might be said to be 'ham'. Would you agree?

2. Which do you think is more important to the Pirate Captain—ham, or his luxurious beard? If you had to choose which was more important to you, which one do you think you would pick?

3. On *The Late Show,* one of the critics, who has a face that looks like it's made of mallow, said to Germaine Greer, 'I wish there were more of Black Bellamy in *The Pirates! In an Adventure with Scientists,* he was the best character ever.' Would you agree with this assessment?

4. Who do you think should play the Pirate Captain if they were ever to make a movie of this book?

5. Do you think the section in Chapter Five when the Pirate Captain forces several pirates to walk the plank is included to show that life at sea had a harsh edge to it? Or do you think the author has some other motives?

6. Choose the letter that best represents your feelings: 'Upon completion of *The Pirates! In an Adventure with Scientists,* I would describe my mood as ____________

(A) angry (B) restless (C) excitable
(D) sleepy (E) afraid

7. Scientifically speaking, who do you think the tallest pirate in the world is?

THANK YOU

WORDS TO KNOW

lubber	pirate	starboard
ham	sloop	galley

ACKNOWLEDGEMENTS

First, to Richard Murkin, because this book is the product of us knocking about for the last ten years. Thanks also to Helen Garnons-Williams for her ace editing, Claire Paterson for her ace agenting, and Caitlin Moran for actually sending it to Claire in the first place. I should mention that David Cordingly's *Life Among the Pirates* and Bodenstandig 2000's *Maxi German Rave Blast Hits 3* both came in very useful when I was writing this.

Plus (for a load of different reasons) my mum, Sam Brown, Chloe Brown, Rob Adey, Nicola Hughes, Dr. Jack Button, Danny Garlick, Sherhan Lingham, and Rebecca Andrews. And Ruth.

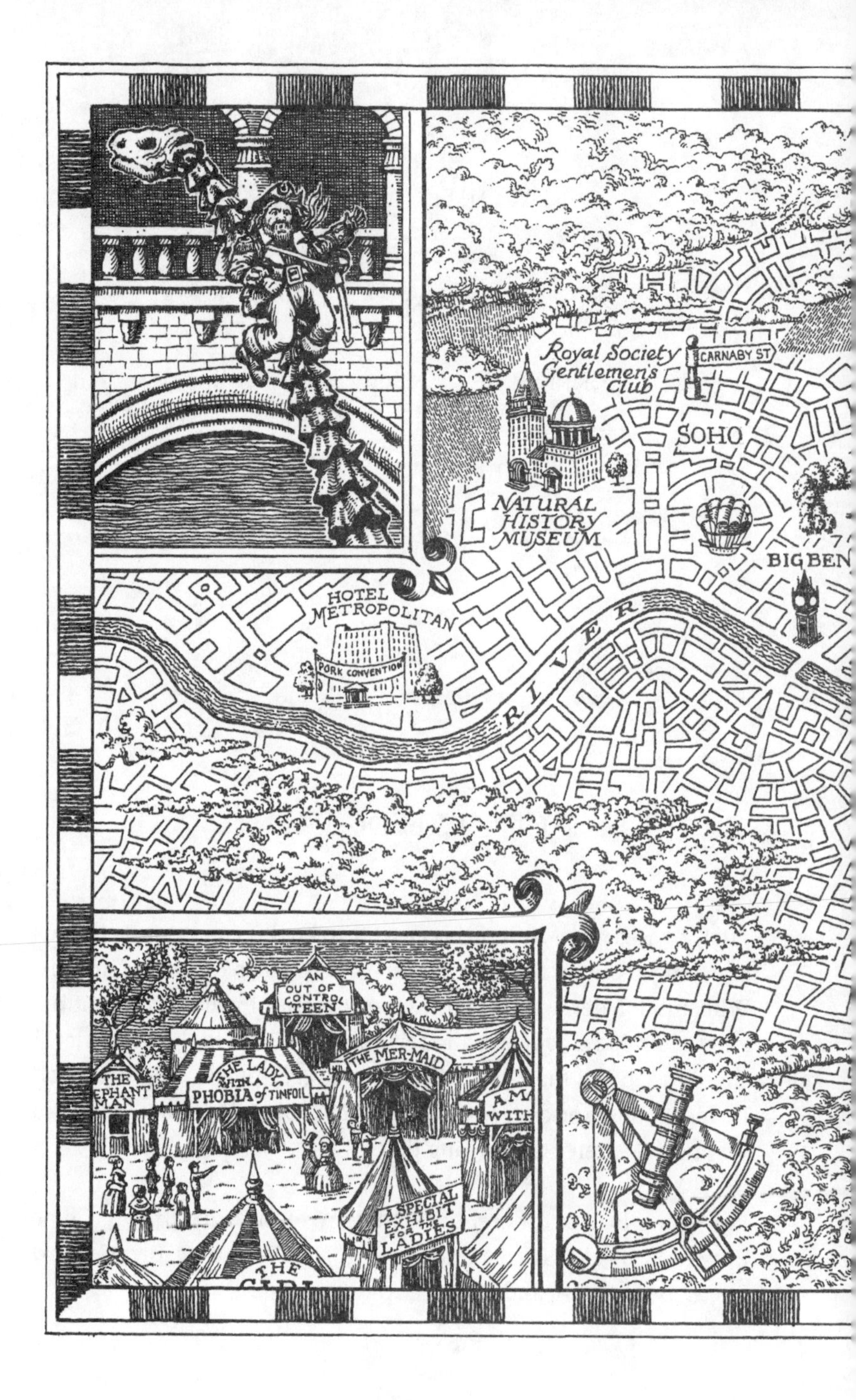
Royal Society
Gentlemen's
Club
CARNABY ST
SOHO
NATURAL
HISTORY
MUSEUM
BIG BEN
HOTEL
METROPOLITAN
PORK CONVENTION
RIVER
AN
OUT OF
CONTROL
TEEN
THE MER-MAID
THE LADY
WITH A
PHOBIA of TINFOIL
A SPECIAL
EXHIBIT
FOR THE
LADIES
THE

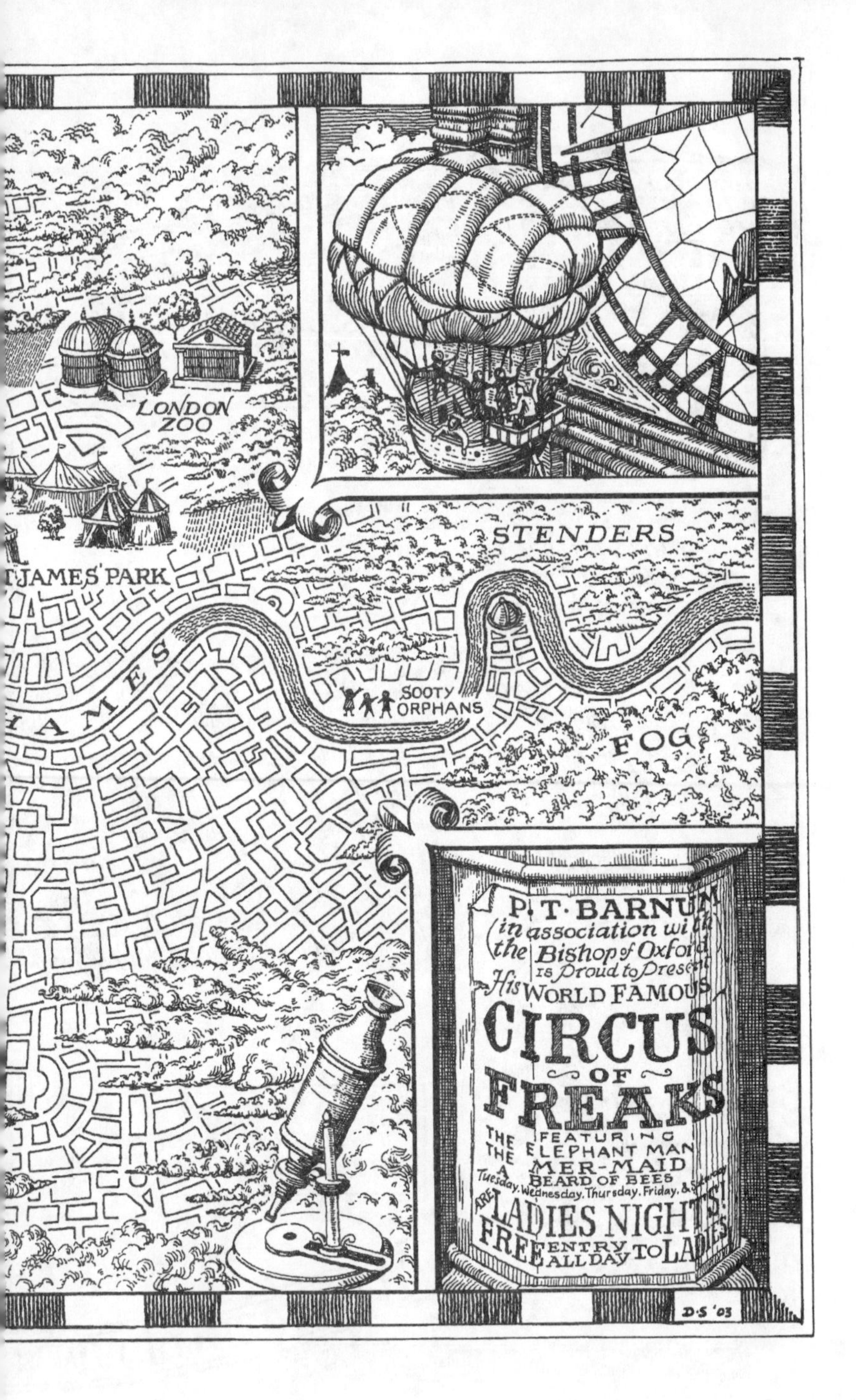
LONDON ZOO
T JAMES' PARK
STENDERS
SOOTY ORPHANS
FOG
P·T·BARNUM
(in association wi
the Bishop of Oxfo
is Proud to Pres
His WORLD FAMOU
CIRCUS
OF
FREAKS
FEATURING
THE ELEPHANT MAN
THE MER-MAID
A BEARD OF BEES
Tuesday, Wednesday, Thursday, Friday, &
ARE LADIES NIGHT
FREE ENTRY ALL DAY TO LA
D·S '03

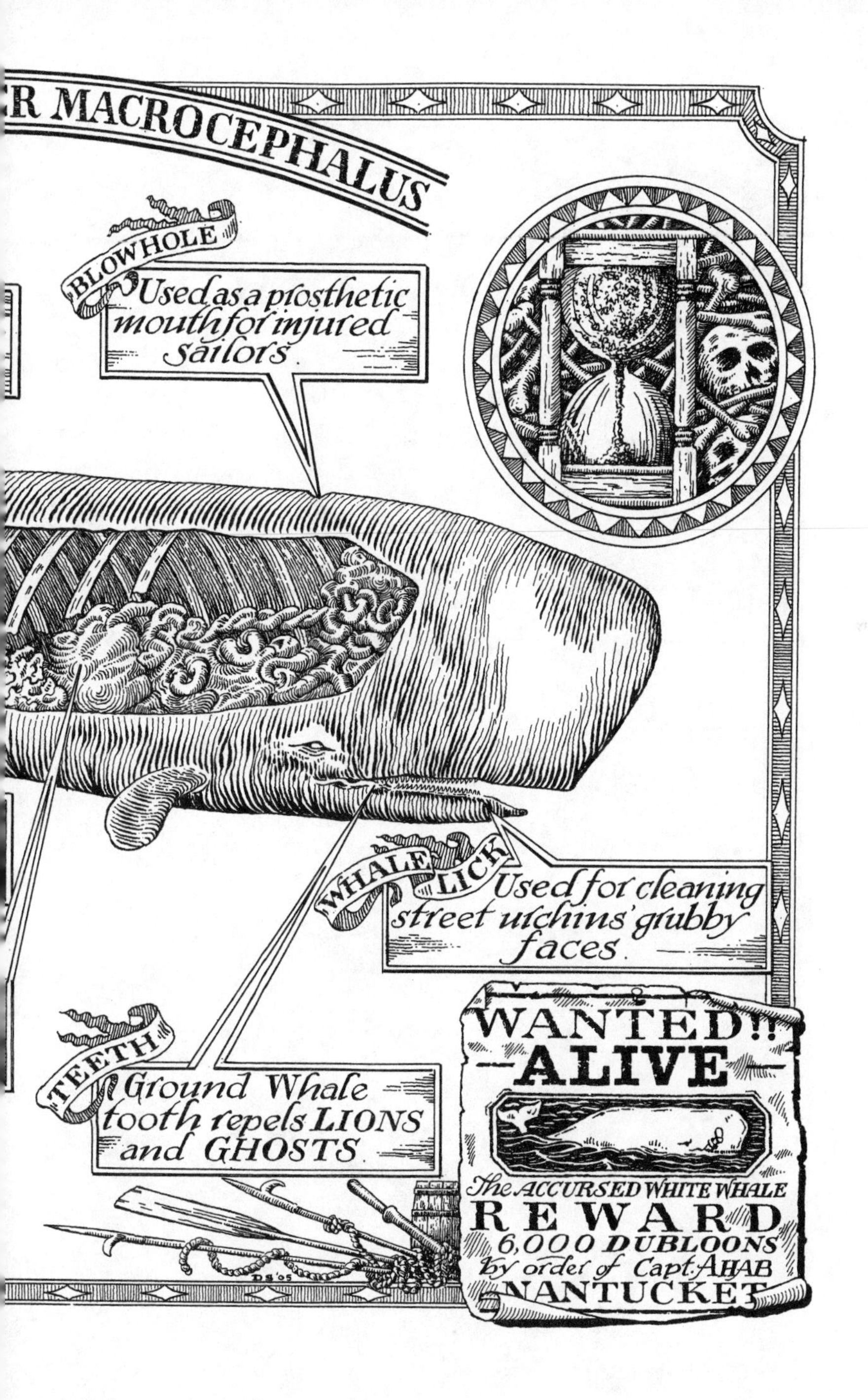
R MACROCEPHALUS
BLOWHOLE
Used as a prosthetic mouth for injured sailors.
WHALE LICK
Used for cleaning street urchins' grubby faces.
TEETH
Ground Whale tooth repels LIONS and GHOSTS.
WANTED!! ALIVE
The ACCURSED WHITE WHALE
REWARD
6,000 DUBLOONS
by order of Capt. AHAB
NANTUCKET
DS '05